PRAISE FOR TED NUGENT

"We're glad you're here. You are a good man."
—*President George W. Bush*

"It gives me great pleasure to personally commend Ted's efforts to preserve and promote our proud sportsmen's heritage. His attention and unwavering devotion to the needs and best interests of the sporting community aligns him with those who exemplify the founding principles of this great nation."
—*Tom Ridge, Director, Office of Homeland Security*

"I appreciate all Ted does in support of the Second Amendment. Our adversaries never let up, and neither can we."
—*Congressman Bob Barr of Georgia*

"We are proud of Mr. Nugent's contributions to his profession, and to our state. His involvement should inspire others to greater awareness and action."
—*Governor John Engler of Michigan*

"I thank Ted so much for his continued friendship and support. I cannot tell you what that means to me."
—*Tommy G. Thompson, Secretary of Health and Human Services*

Kill It & Grill It

"Our Spiritual BBQ"

—Ted & Shemane Nugent

TED & SHEMANE NUGENT
Kill It & Grill It

A Guide to
PREPARING and COOKING
WILD GAME and FISH

Since 1947
REGNERY
PUBLISHING, INC.
An Eagle Publishing Company • Washington, DC

Library of Congress Cataloging-in-Publication Data

Nugent, Ted.
Kill it and grill it : a guide to preparing and cooking
wild game and fish / Ted and Shemane Nugent.
p. cm.
ISBN 0-89526-164-2
ISBN 0-89526-036-0 (paperback)
1. Cookery (Game) 2. Hunting.
I. Nugent, Shemane. II. Title.
TX751 .N84 2002
641.6'91—dc21

2002000625

First paperback edition published in 2005

Published in the United States by
Regnery Publishing, Inc.
An Eagle Publishing Company
One Massachusetts Avenue, NW
Washington, DC 20001

Visit us at www.regnery.com

Manufactured in the United States of America

10 9 8 7 6 5 4 3

Books are available in quantity for promotional or premium use.
Write to Director of Special Sales, Regnery Publishing, Inc.,
One Massachusetts Avenue, NW, Washington, DC 20001,
for information on discounts and terms or call (202) 216-0600.

*Dedicated to the great American families
who celebrate hands-on environmental awareness
in the grand and honorable culture of
hunting, fishing, and trapping,
thereby guaranteeing balanced biodiversity.*

SOME FOLKS MIGHT REMEMBER that George Bernard Shaw—a sandal-wearing socialist vegetarian—tried to reform the spelling of the English language. Big deal. Big musty flop. This book—by the hard-drivin', hard-lovin', full-throbbin', high-octane, deerslayin', allthings-scarin', ballistic guitarboy—*Nugetizes* it. Get ready to rock, doc.

CONTENTS

INTRODUCTION
Celebrate the Flesh

P RAISE AND BRAISE THE FLESH! Wild game meat has no equal. Tribe Nuge has not bought domestic flesh since 1969, and the quality of our average meal is nothing short of awe inspiring. Venison is the term generally used to describe deer flesh, but it includes all wild flesh, be it fowl, herbivore, or carnivore, large or small. Backstrap fever comes in many forms. We celebrate the delicious, natural, pure, organic, high-protein, no-fat, low-cholesterol dynamo of elk, deer, moose, caribou, buffalo, antelope, gemsbok, kudu, impala, eland, hartebeest, dik-dik, steinbok, duiker, hyala, bushbuck, reedbuck, cougar, bear, duck, goose, pheasant, quail, dove, grouse, woodcock, snipe, squirrel, rabbit, woodchuck, beaver, wild hog, and other gifts of renewable sustenance with vigor. It is good to know exactly where one's food comes from. Hands-on cause-and-effect provides valuable lessons in environmental responsibility. You can't deny a gutpile.

There is no trick in preparing game for the table. If every step of the hunt is taken to heart, from the intense studying and understanding of wildlife, through marksmanship proficiency and woodsmanship skills, right on down to the gutting and butchering of game, that dedication will form a lasting bond that produces a certain respect and value for this life-giving commodity. The cycle works, and there is no pretending or avoiding it. Sharpen them knives, and celebrate the Spirit of the Wild!

Clean, cold, and fresh. Those are the three magic ingredients for a perfect meal. Cleaning the carcass properly in the field; keeping it as cool as possible before aging, cooking, or freezing; and serving it in a timely manner are the keys to quality premium tablefare. If these steps are followed, heaven will be on your dinner plate and in your gut.

Conscientious intelligent fieldcare is the first step, and diligent care must be taken to remove all entrails and body fluids efficiently and thoroughly. Plenty of books and videos are available in the marketplace to show blow-by-blow detail, but there is still no better lesson than hands-on by an experienced master. Be sure to taste the master's game meals before you conclude his mastership. Then proceed slowly. Take care. And common sense will steer you properly.

Aging game in a cold environment is always a good idea—between 33 and 40 degrees Fahrenheit is best; 35 is perfect. Only pork and bear call for limited hanging. Deer and smallgame will benefit greatly from the aging process and become more tender and tasty with time. A few days—but ten or more is better—is enough time to break down the enzymes and bring out the wonderful and unique flavors that excite us all.

Once family-sized portions are cut, any recipe will do. From the simple to the elaborate, each concoction will bring different taste sensations to every meal. The real trick with game is to NEVER OVERCOOK! Here's a simple example: Pick a flesh, any flesh. Cook slowly over hot coals, but elevated away from intense heat. We use Mexican mesquite, oak, cherry, and hickory coals made of half seasoned and half green wood to keep the smoke coming. Baste and brush with a goop made from butter, olive oil, brown sugar, seasonings, and preserves of your choice (our favorites are raspberry and apricot). By constantly brushing the yummy slop onto the meat, we can determine when a nice singed crust is formed while keeping the inside rare and juicy. This works for wild pork and most other wild critters. Bear should be cooked slightly more, but don't cook bear to the core. Oftentimes we add a good mustard and honey to the baste as well. Let your imagination be your guide. If a grill is not available, a roasting pan with everything added at once including the baste—cooked at 450 degrees and basted regularly—will work just fine. (We follow the same procedure with sliced peppers, potatoes, rutabagas, turnips, eggplant, celery, asparagus, earcorn, apples, squash, and onions.)

With each stroke of the basting brush and with every turn of each piece of food, exciting flashes of the hunt and ever-stimulating animal encounters come flooding forth. Each wind is relived. Every wild birdsong re-echoes. The pulse quickens as if the shot were about to take place again. When one responsibly procures his family's dinner by hand, each meal becomes a sacred rite, and the reality of life and death is undeniable. It is good, and so is the feast.

1

I KILL IT, I GRILL IT

Slabbage. Haunch. Shank. Incredible edible Carcai. Flesh Gritz. SoulFood. Dinner on the hoof. FairChase BBQ. HumpChow. Pissed-off protein. I kill it, I grill it. It's my life. I live to eat and eat to live. I live to hunt and hunt to live. The essence of life is getting food. Goodfood. Sacred food. It's all so simple, it's stupid.

Vegetarians are cool. All I eat are vegetarians—except for the occasional mountain lion steak. Pure, real, honest-to-God free-range protein is the rocketfuel for my spiritual campfire. Free-range chicken aint free and that aint no range. Venison is freerange. Pheasant is freerange. The almighty Ruffed Grouse is freerange. I'm freerange. Chickens are incarcerated; some are more feces pecking, deathrow toxic than others. They'll never be a mezmerizing, exploding, gaudyass flushing swampchicken on a soul-cleansing frosty November morn, erupting from a nostril-punching sawgrass marsh, giving my Labrador retriever,

Gonzo the WonderDog, and me a full predator spiritual erection. If it can't get away, it aint freerange, and I aint interested. Period.

My quality of life is directly attributable to the number of bar-b-ques my family, friends, and I celebrate. My sacred grilltime can best be described as a spiritual BBQ orgy of the senses. We don't just cook—we dance naked at the primordial campfire of life. We don't just eat—we celebrate each and every stimulating mouthful of precious life-giving chow. And we sure as hell wouldn't waste good hunger or any one of our much anticipated family mealtimes on fastfood or junkfood. Nosireebob. At the Nugent tribal dinnertable we think of fastfood as a mallard or quail, garlic'd and buttered to perfection. Our tastebuds are the second most important nerve endings in our lives, and the only nerve endings we actually share as a family. The other ones are reserved for proper, private affairs of the spirit and flesh between consenting adults, before and after the dining fleshfest. The Physics of Spirituality for the soul.

The way we eat, I can't believe my wife, kids, and I don't weigh a thousand pounds apiece. Then again, it's the intellectual care we put forth feeding ourselves such balanced purity that causes us to be ultraconscientious and aware of our overall health. We take these gifts from God very, very seriously, and demand quality fuel for the beast within. That's why we dine exclusively on fresh deadstuff in the first place. Birth, hunt, sex, food, rock 'n' roll, death. Itsa damn party. Don't dick around.

In a world of laughable cultural disconnect and embarrassing and anti-intellectual vacuousness, I am compelled more and more to be ultimately self-sufficient and fiercely independent as a hunter. Apathy and roomservice are for sheep and wimps. Some try to tell me that I don't need to hunt. Well, I don't need to grow my own vegetables either—there are a million cans on the shelves if I want veggies. And of course I don't need to play the guitar either—there are unlimited recordings of others who play the guitar. Some claim I don't need to cut my own wood or plant my own trees. Goofballs squawk that I don't need to kill my food because there are already nicely wrapped packages of meat at the grocery store. And of course, I probably don't need to breed with my wife, as some see it, for certainly I could find someone else to do these things for me. Bullshit. You don't need tofu or gurus either, but go nuts. Just leave me and my natural world alone, thank you.

The most astonishing example of this outrageous excuse-making denial cult is an exchange I had on the ABC radio show of my friend Sean Hannity of the *Hannity & Colmes* Fox News TV program. Sean's a great man representing truth and honesty whenever he opens his mouth. He's my BloodBrother and I respect him much. As I prepared for this American Dream day on tour for yet another soul-cleansing night of outlando sonic bombast and loud over-the-top R&B outrage with my virtuoso bandmates, soul-brothers bassist-vocalist Marco Mendoza and drummer-vocalist Tommy Clufetos in Kansas City, I channel surfed onto Sean Hannity broadcasting live on Fox News from his radio studios in NYC. It was the glowrious Fourth of July, and Sean was sharing more self-evident truth with his millions of radio listeners and TV viewers. His heartfelt appreciation and celebration of this great nation of ours on Independence Day resonated patriotism and goodwill. Sharing the TV screen with Sean was a group of professional chefs from downtown Manhattan, poking and turning over beautiful slabs of nicely singed, grilled flesh of assorted species and origins. The properly butchered body parts of chickens, pigs, sheep, and cattle graced the smoking grills on the TV screen, certainly accurately representing this day—like most summer days in America—with literally hundreds of millions of grills across the land putting fire to the flesh of billions upon billions of dead critters to feed the good families celebrating this most important of days. How better to give honor to life, liberty, and the pursuit of happiness than to party hardy with delicious meat, lovingly carved from the skeletons of protein-rich animals in their ultimate afterlife habitat of steel and charcoal? (Excuse me while I wipe the corners of my mouth.) I had hunting buddies waiting for me at the Bonner Springs Amphitheater for our own BBQ feast-o-flesh, so my spirit was soaring.

Assisting Sean was his longtime secretary, Flipper. That's right, her name is Flipper, like the trained dolphin on the Disney Channel. Ol' Flipper and I had a little point-counterpoint gitdown only a month or so earlier, when she called me a savage murderer, or some such, because I "murdered" little, innocent, defenseless creatures like Bambi. I tried to explain to her that real flesh-and-blood, living animals are not at all like cartoon characters, but, of course, with a name like Flipper, I have a funny feeling that discomforting reality didn't get through to her. Her fantasy was like Kevlar body armor for the brain. She didn't get it at all.

I picked up the phone and decided to give Sean a call, as I have a standing invitation to join him on his program anytime I can. Sean greeted me enthusiastically, and I commenced to give him a vibrant energized update from the wonderful world of our Full Bluntal Nugity 2001 Tour from the heartland. I simply offered my sincere salute to the brave men and women of law enforcement and the armed forces to which my first book, *God, Guns, and Rock 'n' Roll*, was dedicated, and offered a heartfelt thanx to all my workin' hard, playin' hard American friends for all the years of support and intense enthusiasm for my long, crazed, gravity-defying career. Of course I emphasized the importance of Fox News offering BBQ tips on their network as everybody across America was literally having one huge continental grillfest and could always use some advice on how to better handle and conduct the traditional cookout.

Knowing good radio when he hears it, Sean decided to bring on Flipper so she could find fault with all this fiery flesh being consumed across the land. She came on squawking as usual, with her ridiculous condemnation of murder and slaughter and violence and hate, somehow believing that the idea of cooking flesh was some weird horror uniquely mine. But the beauty of it was when she desperately scrambled, live on the radio to millions of BBQ devotees, to justify her choice of "freerange chicken" as a food-source that, according to her, somehow didn't include any killing. She went on to say how I was this heartless heathen for killing pheasant and deer to feed my family. Even as I tried to explain how her eating a dead chicken was patent, undeniable authorization on her part to the act of killing said chicken, and, therefor, killing of animals for food in general, she held fast to her unbelievable denial. She wasn't going for it. She adamantly insisted how her paying for the death and eating of the chicken was not her authorization or acceptance of the act of killing it for her dinner. Can you believe that? She ranted on and on about how she didn't kill anything. Her chicken was "free and natural." She couldn't and certainly wouldn't kill anything. Her denial was so deep, it was hysterical. I can only imagine that she was a huge Grateful Dead fan and quite possibly, allegedly, may have used some of the same mind-altering chemicals the deadheads needed in order to be fans of that soulless, out of tune, zero-feeling country and western pap they forced out of their instruments and into the altered minds of their tie-dyed airheads. High on cocaine indeed. There really can't be any other explanation, allegedly.

NUGE
**RECIPE FOR
THE SOUL
AND GUTS**
by Chef Nuge

**Kill legal game.
Add fire.
Devour.
Thank you,
drive safely!**

We wrapped up the interview, with Sean incredulous that his own assistant could be so stupid and shallow, and I reveled in the fact that she was the ultimate foil for my prohunting, pro-omnivorous lifestyle. She represented the animal rights and antihunting lunatic fringe perfectly. I could not have hired, trained, and scripted anyone to better represent the critics of hunting or meat eating in general than Flipper babe. I cannot thank her enuf. I went on that night to perform one hellofa firebreathing rockout, fueled by singed venison, the Great Spirit of the Wild by which I procured it, the BloodBrother campfire backstage, and the phenomenal ignorance and idiocy of Flipper and her ilk of denial. I didn't floss or wipe the greaze from my fingers before the concert, hoping to get maximum mileage from the natural oils of the beast that provided me energy and fuel that night, straight to my guitarstrings for optimal tone and attitude. My God the music was Xtra sexy as the sun fell beneath the western horizon and twenty thousand people danced the BBQ dance with me. The GREAT WHITE BUFFALO ran Xtra wild that night. Well done. ✘

How better to give honor
to life, liberty, and the
pursuit of happiness than
to party hardy with
delicious meat, lovingly
carved from the skeletons
of protein-rich animals in
their ultimate afterlife
habitat of steel and
charcoal?

2

CELEBRATING THRIVING WILDLIFE

My eyes virtually bugged out of my face, little rivulets of drool forming at the corner of my trembling mouth. I hyperventilated. My heartbeat and pulse thumped like a hyper speed-metal rock 'n' roll double bassdrum from hell, and the hair on my arms and neck quivered and rose to the occasion. The sheer outrageous sea of hornage before me was beyond my wildest big game dreams. Along with hundreds of families from around the world, I was staring at four walls covered with the most beautiful, stunning mounted heads of the world's largest deer, elk, moose, buffalo, caribou, antelope, muskoxen, bighorn sheep, cougar, and grizzly, polar, and black bears ever seen in a single setting. This was the forty-year anniversary of the Pope & Young Club biannual trophy awards recording session, and a grand celebratory spirit consumed the Salt Lake City Convention Center. The Spirit of the Wild glowed all around.

Numerous new world records had once again been broken, and we all knew why. Since the inception of scientifically based wildlife management, begun at the insistence of hunters in the late 1800s, big game populations have improved exponentially year after year.

The evidence is inescapable. Recordbook deer, elk, bear, moose, buffalo, antelope, caribou, cougar, and other game prove conclusively that this incredibly disciplined, ultraselective, trophy-hunting community performs the ultimate benefit for wildlife populations. In order to qualify for the Boone & Crockett, Pope & Young, or various state record-keeping organizations, a big game animal must be healthy and in almost every instance, very old. And in the animal world, very old equates to being beyond breeding capability or providing any tangible benefit to the herd. In most cases, older male specimens are banished from the herd and go off on their own to die a slow, agonizing death by starvation or by being eaten alive by other predators. It is interesting to note as well that most older critters that would set new world records are never encountered by hunters and vanish without a trace. I for one am glad that so many are taken by hunters not only for the thrills and challenges of the hunt and the food they provide the hunters' families, plus incredible sums of revenues generated via these hunts, but most importantly for the valuable data they have provided over the years for further and better management information. Even in death, these majestic beasts benefit the wild, their species, and mankind. Celebrate the Great Spirit!

Thanks to the Rocky Mountain Elk Foundation, Ducks Unlimited, the Foundation for North American Wild Sheep, the National Wild Turkey Federation, Whitetails Forever Network,

Pheasants Forever, the Ruffed Grouse Society, Quail Unlimited, Trout Unlimited, the White-Tail and Mule Deer Association, and so many other conservation organizations dedicated to these precious renewable wildlife resources, it is very easy to see why wildlife is thriving in North America like nowhere else in the world. (See Appendix for directory of these and other conservation organizations.) Even in the face of dramatically dwindling habitat, game and nongame species are doing great because these hunting organizations' hands-on understanding of real wildlife needs and conditions drive us to manage habitat and harvests accordingly. Many wildlife lovers outside the hunting community join us in this glowing success story. Even the TV personality Steve Irwin, "The Crocodile Hunter," has said that habitat destruction is the most important issue facing his home country of Australia—as well as America and the world. Those who walk on the wildside know this truth. I repeat: wildlife habitat is where our air, soil, and water quality come from. Everybody should be helping these hunting organizations. If intellectual truth instead of emotional hysteria motivated everyone, they would.

Those ignorant souls who criticize and condemn "trophy hunters" are absolutely full of baloney. First of all, most trophy animals are taken by chance, as a rare lucky encounter with an outsized beast. And in virtually every case, dictated by laws and standard hunters' ethics, all the valuable meat is utilized before the head is taken to the wildlife artist taxidermist. The facts are clear. The literally thousands of entries every year into many record books around the country obviously represent only a minor fraction of the overall annual harvest of all species. That reality adds up to an amazing dynamic truth about just how renewable these resources truly are. Isn't it ridiculous that anyone believes there

TED NUGENT
ESSENCE OF LIFE GONZO RECIPE

1—Go hunting, breathe deep, feel the air, take the Spirit inside, and kill a critter.

2—Remove the hair. Take out the guts. Immediately clean and cool the carcass. Butcher flesh into family-sized portions.

3—Start fire. Heat good fresh vegetable oil to boiling point in an iron skillet.

4—Fill zipbag with flour, salt and pepper, and good seasoning mixture. Add small, manageable chunks of meat; shake and slide coated pieces into hot oil to sizzle.

5—As brown crust forms on edges, remove onto paper towel. Salivate. Surround yourself with family and friends. Put on plates next to smashed potatoes with skins on. Cut, eat, grin, sip Vernor's Ginger Ale, burp, enjoy.

could even be an antihunting argument? You would have to be pretty darn stupid to deny more than one hundred years of consistent evidence. But then there have always been stupid people. I can only hope that they wake up and smell the wonderful, gargantuan field of roses that shines before them. I often wonder just what they are trying to accomplish. I guess weird will always be weird.

Meanwhile, I am going to continue to support all these great hunting/conservation groups. They work tirelessly throughout the year raising millions and millions of dollars, donated by millions and millions of hunters across the land, all for the continued benefit of wildlife and wildlife habitat. It is truly the greatest wildlife success story in the history of the world. When I travel to Africa, for example, it is so very obvious how it all works. Where I see thriving populations of elephant, rhino, hippo, lion, leopard, cheetah, Cape buffalo, kudu, eland, sable, gemsbok, giraffe, warthog, impala, zebra, wildebeest, nyala, reedbuck, klipspringer, blesbok, bontebok, tsessebe, duiker, steinbok, and all those fascinating wild creatures, it is always on wildground where legal hunting is an ongoing business. Conversely, where I see no wildlife at all, there are goats, cattle, vineyards, golfcourses, and "No Hunting" signs. Intellectually, the choice is ridiculously obvious, unless, of course, feeling good is more important than doing the right thing. As a hunter who lives with these awesome beasts, I will continue to dedicate my life to educating and motivating people to do the right thing. 🏹

CHAPTER

3

PURE SUSTENANCE— BUTCHER YOUR OWN

Hell, I'm just a guitar player, but even gimpy I know how to reduce a recently dancing critter into delicious, tender, family-sized portions. I remain constantly amazed at how helpless so many people— especially some of my fellow hunters—are out there. People who cannot even gut their animals properly, much less properly butcher them for the table. The greatest compliment ever bestowed upon me was when a drooling animal rights crusader pointed his grimy finger at me and yelled that I was nothing but a "BUTCHER!" Yikes! Thank you very much, tofu breath. Professional butchers are essential talented providers of our communities, now more than ever according to the most recent reports of increased meat in America's diet. The high-protein health diet craze is a sensible return to a more effective, well-balanced diet. Life is a BBQ.

I was originally inspired to learn basic butchering because I didn't trust the local meat cutter to safely return my own precious venison that had made its way to the Nuge table with so much effort, difficulty, and so much extra time and attention taken to handle with special care in the field. What goes into my family's mouths and bodies is serious stuff where I come from. Balanced with the love that feeds our spirit, nothing could be more important.

If we really give a royal hoot, we would monitor more closely the step-by-step process by which our food goes from living, breathing beast to cookable, digestible portions. Same goes for veggies and fruits. If we knew the horrid ingredients of the pesticides and herbicides and feces that coat our produce, we would demand an immediate halt to the mass poisoning. And we sure as hell wouldn't continue the standard operating procedure of feeding rotted, diseased carcasses back to the livestock we consume, now would we? I'd be a madcow, too. The MotorCity Mad-CowMan. Scary.

The killing of game for consumption is a deep, intensely connecting act. To take an animal's life in order to feed our family is serious, serious stuff. We must elevate the meaning of this activity to a much higher level in our lives. I believe the hunting and killing procedure has been cheapened, too often by too many, to a mere recreational maneuver. It is, in fact, much more than that. The stress reduction that takes place in the outdoors—pursuing game, breathing, touching, and soulfully harmonizing with the primal scream of self-sufficiency—is undeniable but far from the top of the motivational list in most hunters' hearts. Though often-times more than 99 percent of our hunt time is, in fact, seeking and not killing, the mindset to kill, nonetheless, is the primary and most powerful impulse surrounding the overall hunting endeavor. This is no bird-watching walk in the woods.

So when flesh is brought to bag, the sacred ritual of butchering must be optimized to truly show respect for this life-giving gift. And the right way is quite simple. Use the many great books and videos on the market that give illustrations for fieldcare and transportation procedures to maximize the quality of wild meat from heap to haunch. There is too much gross negligence in the hunting camps of this country, and I would encourage, if not outright beg, for a massive crusade to educate each other on the proper handling of this most precious stuff. Review, review, review. Share, discuss, and demand.

The simplest way I can describe my own meat handling procedure is to say: kill, clean, cool, cut, cure, freeze, and rejoice.

KILL—The first clean we must embrace is the clean kill. A quick, efficient death will produce better meat, period. This is where the thrilling marksmanship challenge must be taken to heart to become absolutely proficient with our chosen weapon. Hit em square behind the shoulder, forward into the heart and lungs of the inner chest, for an instant kill, whether with bow or firearm. Then track that animal and get to work. By avoiding major skeletal bones, our projectile will not only disrupt less edible meat, but our hit will cause less hydrostatic shock, therefor reducing the ensuing adrenaline dumpage. It is this explosion of endorphins and adrenaline that can taint the overall taste of game meat. So avoid that big shoulder blade if you can.

CLEAN—The edible flesh must be cleaned thoroughly and kept clean throughout the process. In remote conditions, wet grasses or other clean vegetation can be used to wipe the cavity and meat after all viscera is removed. It is important to get all the blood and body fluids away from the flesh. When accessible, a good hosing out with fresh, cold, clean water is a good idea. Hanging the kill by the head will expedite the draining process.

COOL—Hunting is just plain cool, but the carcass must be kept good and cold until consumption or freezing. Removing the hide and propping open the body cavity will help dissipate the damaging heat from inside, but unless the air temperature is below 40 degrees, the meat must immediately be hung in a refrigerated cooler or butchered. On remote campsites, skinned and hung in the shade will usually do the trick as long as the carcass is heavily peppered and covered in a cheesecloth gamebag. (A great product is LIQUID GAMEBAG, (307)789-5832, out of Wyoming, that protects and preserves meat in the outback.) We have also experienced positive results by hanging the carcass in a constant flow of woodsmoke. But get that meat to a cooler if the temperature rizes.

CUT—At this point the liver, heart, tenderloins, and backstraps can be cooked and consumed outright because these prime cuts do not necessarily need to be aged or cured, and taste fantastic right off. Even other cuts of flesh can now be reduced to thin, one- or two-inch strips to be made into biltong for great eating.

If traditional packages of meat are preferred, family-sized portions must now be determined for wrapping and freezing. Rule #1 for game meat is to remove all fat, cartilage, and silver membrane. Even fowl has a sour tasting fat, and all white tallow and filmy membrane must be cut away and given to the dogs and cats. One exception is wild pork fat, which is quite sweet and delicious.

I prefer to bone out all our meat, eliminating any sawing that could cause bone particles to taint the flesh. Basically I follow the contour of the muscles and body parts, cutting through to the bone and sectioning each steak away from the skeleton. I have experienced great success by trial and error, but good diagrams and instructions are readily available in book, brochure, and video format. Basic beef butchering cuts work quite well on all game.

CURE—The old world biltong or jerky system of meat curing is simple, effective, and delicious, and any source of clean meat can be made this way: The meat is placed in a brine solution made of vinegar, salt, pepper, and any preferred seasonings, and soaked overnight. Then the strips are hung in warm sunny conditions to air dry. An oven can suffice if the weather is not conducive. As long as all the moisture is removed, these strips last a long, long time and provide good eating without refrigeration. Of course smoking is an option in lieu of the air-drying for a more distinct flavorful curing.

FREEZE—Being ever certain to remove all blood and hair, I tightly double wrap or vacuum seal my family's packages for individual meals in good quality freezer paper. Each package is clearly labeled in black marker identifying the animal, cut, and date. This procedure has become a grand tradition in the Nugent family, where the entire tribe gathers together to clean, trim, wrap, and label packages of this precious commodity. It is an especially valuable lesson for the children as they learn hands-on where life comes from. I believe it is an essential ritual that all families should practice.

REJOICE—It is a grand feeling when you retrieve a package of meat from the freezer that was so intimately handled and cared for every step of the way. You know for certain that it's pure, healthy, and primo quality. Zero chance of e-coli or salmonella when such infinite care is taken to monitor the very process of your family's sustenance. You will read the label on that package and smile with powerful memories of the original encounter with the beast as if it had just happened all over again. And isn't that how it should be? It should. 🏹

Biltong Jerky

First step, kill something! Age it appropriately in the proper clean, cold environment—ideally 33 to 40 degrees for up to one week or even ten days, thus letting the amino acids reduce for more tender, delicious chow. With venison and other wild game flesh, remove all silver membrane and white fat. (I don't waste this precious commodity. I feed it to my cats, dogs, and songbirds.) Slice a couple of pounds of lean meat into 1-inch-wide strips about 5 inches long and ¼-inch thick (they should fit in a heavy duty Ziploc bag). Marinate them overnight in a covered glass dish in a good, commercial marinade (we like Allegro) OR create a concoction of apple cider vinegar, soy sauce, garlic salt, and seasoned pepper. Rinse strips thoroughly with cold water and pat dry. Dry the strips on a cookie sheet in a 140 degree oven with the door open slightly to release steam, for about 8 hours or till the strips are pliable but not brittle. I use a smoker unit on our deck to flavor the meat slowly, using a combination of green and seasoned hickory and apple wood with Mexican mesquite chips. I keep the meat away from direct heat and allow the smoke to do its magic overnight. Inexpensive, small smoking units are available at most sport shops. I store my biltong in the fridge till I pack em up for a day in the treestand, roadtrips, sport events, school games, or an adventure of a lifetime. Eat meat. Live good. Survive! Thrive!

4

BACKSTRAP FEVER

The meaning of life is to be alive. And ya gotta eat. We as a species are still here for the simple reason that we progressed onward in time fueled by the immaculate protein, spirit, and attitude of flesh. If mankind is anything, we surely are hunters. Those who think otherwise are either ultimate Grateful Dead fans, goofy, or in pathetic, terminal Gomer denial. The evidence is irrefutable and everywhere. One would have to intentionally hide from this truth to not get it. I, for one, celebrate it on a daily basis. We don't take meals lightly at the Nugent Camp. Each meal is a celebration of the flesh as the ultimate conveyor of the spirit. Tastebuds, like all wonderful nerve endings, are made to be stimulated and caressed. My mouth craves intensity. The junk that passes as fastfood in America is an embarrassment. My idea of fastfood is a hardstroking passing mallard or a pissed-off elk. My daily quality of life is determined by how happy my palette can be found at any given moment. Zest is what I eat. Flavor is my high. If it weren't for real butter, I wouldn't have no luck at all. The only thing I like fat free are my womenfolk. Which brings us to the maincourse.

I thank the Good Lord each day for the season-o-harvest and deerhunting in America. Prowling the deepest game-infested wilds of at least six or seven states each fall and winter, my trail of bloody arrows and steaming gutpiles is matched only by the stunned whitefolk in the afterglow aftermath aftershock of my dangerass hi-velocity R&B MotorCity guitarstorm. It's the least I can do to my fellow Americans. With an average deerkill in excess of fifty animals per annum, we certainly do celebrate the mighty protein of venison. Now, mind you, each and every critter is legally accounted for and nary a scrap of sacred flesh would ever be allowed to go to waste. And as much as Tribe Nuge loves our mesquite BBQ, we can only eat so much of anything in good conscience. So, you ask, where the hell does all that meat go? Well I'll tell you, salmonella breath, it goes to my neighbors, family, employees, friends, acquaintances; and through the wonderful Hunters for the Hungry program, Farmers and Hunters Feeding the Hungry, Sportsmen Against Hunger, and numerous other sporter-funded charities, this precious life-giving commodity is channeled into the ultimate and beneficial utilization by being processed and donated to the needy. Hand-in-hand with my fellow Ted Nugent United Sportsmen of America members, Safari Club International, Michigan Bow Hunters, Michigan United Conservation Clubs, Pheasants Forever, Whitetails Unlimited, and many more American hunting groups across the fruited hinterland, we provide millions and millions of highly desirable, hot, delicious, quality meals to millions of needy, hungry Americans each year. I personally have improved habitat, increased herds, killed many surplus deer, gutted, skinned, butchered, cooked, and served up wonderful chow to many in my hometown of Detroit and elsewhere and will continue to do so because it is the right thing to do. And do they ever appreciate it!

Regardless of the obvious generosity of so many sporters, there is an element of stinginess that cannot be denied. All of the haunch that I donate is premium quality venison for sure. But I cannot tell a lie. Ma Nuge didn't raise no fool. I keep all the sacred backstrap for ourselves. Top-o-the-loin. That spectacular delicate strip of pure brown meat that resides along the backbone of deer, elk, moose, caribou, antelope, buffalo, and all herbivores and bovine and mountain lions, too. The filet mignon. Ribeye. What many label as tenderloin, but it aint. The tenderloin is a smaller tube of steak that is found inside the body cavity just forward of the pelvic bone on the underside of the beast. Certainly a delicacy itself and typically consumed the night of the kill, smothered in butter and onions, prepared right along with diced potatoes. Chow fit for kings. Come January, our freezers are wall-to-wall backstrap, and we consume it with sheer abandon and savage appreciation. It is gold. Only a fool would allow this primecut to be included with ground meat or combined in any way with other cuts of meat. Medallions of backstrap singed quick and sizzled up in hot oil with the simplest of batters is a meal to behold. There is no other so delicious, so tantalizing, so pure. We take great care to butcher the strap very carefully, taking pains to remove all the silver and white membrane and all fat from the Kingly Slabbage, and to delicately filet from the backbone and top of the ribs. We get meticulously surgical. Once trimmed and cleaned completely of any possible dirt or hair, each strap is divided into three equal cuts, then dried off and vacuum sealed for freezing.

The ultimate respect for a creature comes in its consumption, thereby completing the natural cycle of life and death, bringing the circle to its fitting continuance. Nobody properly loves and respects a critter more than those of us whose lives are furthered and enriched with their life-giving flesh, before, during, and after the hunt. And the circle shall not be broken. Come the ceremonious unveiling of the Strap, all gather round with giddy anticipation. This is PartyTime with Uncle Ted in all its glowry. With fond, dreamy visions of the big encounter back at the Sacred Hunt, I lovingly slice each strap into half-inch thin medallions of beauty, then slap them through a quick bath of egg and half-and-half cream. These dripping morsels are then dusted in a 50-50 bowl of Jackson Michigan's Drakes FryCrisp batter and flour, enhanced with ample McCormick's garlic salt and garlic pepper. This treated hunk is gently laid into sizzling hot peanut oil for a quick singing on both sides, then set on a paper towel-covered plate to dry for but a moment. At this point, I must fend off the family who are like gnarling, growling, starving dogs. Heaped onto a table with sliced potatoes cooked crisp in the same oil with a glob of white gravy over the whole mess, and what you've got here, my friends, is heaven on earth. Washed down with a slug of your favorite wine or a bubbling mug of Vernor's Ginger Ale, and you have yourself the happiest bowhunting guitarplayer and family in the FreeWorld. BackStrap Fever. Its what I got. Its what I crave. 🏹

Pan Roasted Venison Steak

7 tablespoons unsalted butter
2 1- to 1½-pound boneless venison steaks,
    cut 2 inches thick
Coarse salt and cracked black pepper to taste
Sprigs of fresh watercress for garnish

In small saucepan, melt the butter over low heat. Skim off and discard the milky foam on top. Carefully pour the clarified butter into a large iron skillet, avoiding any milky solids at the bottom of the pan.

Dry the venison steaks thoroughly on paper towels and season both sides with the coarse salt and lots of cracked black pepper.

Heat the clarified butter in a large skillet over low heat. Add the steaks without crowding the skillet and sauté on one side for 3 minutes, until well browned. Turn and sauté on the second side for 3 minutes. Reduce the heat to medium-low and continue cooking for 10 minutes. Turn the steaks and cook for another 10 minutes for rare or 14 minutes for medium. The steaks are done when there is slight resistance to the touch. Transfer the steaks to a carving board and let sit 2 to 3 minutes.

Cut the steaks crosswise into thin slices and place in a decorative pattern on each of six warmed individual serving plates. Garnish with sprigs of fresh watercress and serve at once. Serves 6.

Oven Swiss Venison

½ cup flour
¼ teaspoon garlic powder
1 2-pound, ¾-inch-thick venison steak,
    cut into serving sized portions
2 tablespoons oil
1 16-ounce can diced tomatoes
½ cup finely chopped celery
½ cup finely chopped carrots
¼ cup finely chopped onions
1 teaspoon Worcestershire sauce
2 tablespoons shredded sharp cheese of your choice

Combine flour and garlic powder in a shallow dish. Roll meat in flour mixture, then pound flour into meat. Brown venison in a large skillet with oil over high heat. Place steak in a glass baking dish or casserole dish. Add remaining flour to pan drippings, then add tomatoes (including the juice), celery, carrots, onions, and Worcestershire sauce. Cook, stirring frequently, until thick and bubbly, then pour over meat.

Cover and bake at 350 degrees for 1 hour and 20 minutes. Sprinkle with cheese and return to oven for a few minutes more—just long enough to melt the cheese.

Venison Stroganoff

2 pounds venison steaks, fat trimmed and cut
    into thin strips
3 tablespoons (or more) butter
Fresh mushrooms, sliced
⅓ cup cooking sherry
⅓ cup water
1 envelope Lipton onion soup mix
Dash of garlic salt
Dash of curry powder
1 beef bouillon cube
1 cup sour cream

Brown the venison strips quickly in a large skillet with
the butter and mushrooms. Stir in sherry and ⅓ cup water.
Add the onion soup mix, garlic salt, curry powder, and
bouillon cube. Mix well, cover, and simmer for 30 minutes, stirring every 15 minutes and adding liquid when
necessary, until meat is tender. Just before serving, add
sour cream, increase heat, and cook for 1 minute more.
Serve over rice or noodles. Serves 4 unless Ted's eating
over; then it'll serve 2.

Venison Marinade

Many times this marinade has turned those who usually resist game meat into hard-core proponents of its dining excellence AND the hunt itself!

Marinade
⅓ cup quality cooking oil
½ cup finely minced carrots
½ cup finely minced onions
1½ tablespoons fresh crushed garlic
½ cup finely minced shallots
1 tablespoon parsley
1 teaspoon rosemary
1 teaspoon thyme
2 bay leaves
1 cup white vinegar
1¾ cups white wine
7 cups water
2 tablespoons whole black pepper
¼ cup brown sugar

1 to 2 pounds venison

Heat oil in saucepan and sauté carrots and onions until just soft. Add garlic and shallots and sauté 1 minute—DO NOT BROWN! Add all remaining marinade ingredients and simmer for 30 minutes. Strain and cool marinade before pouring over meat. Place meat in a covered glass dish that allows the liquid to cover the entire piece of meat. Marinate overnight or not more than 7 to 8 hours. Remove the meat from the marinade and cook as you prefer, and gloat with the celebration of the flesh! This marinade yields about 2½ quarts.

Venison in Cream Sauce
by Shemane

Sometimes you're at the right place at the right time, and that's how I acquired this extraordinary recipe for "Venison in Cream Sauce." Several years ago, when Ted had his own morning radio show, the station manager cooked up a dream vacation for listeners who wanted to bask in the sun with the MotorCity MadMan on a Spring Break vacation. The beautiful sapphire waters and white sand beaches of Aruba became our home for a week. The whole family went along for the trip, and it was a wonderful, relaxing vacation. Normally, we don't take vacations unless business is involved; so, this holiday was a welcomed respite. The problem was Aruba, as a very small island, is not a very attractive place for someone like Ted who has an inherent desire to roam forests. Sun bathing and shopping are two of his least favorite activities. There are, however, great restaurants in Aruba, and we came across a quaint little German place that Ted loved. He liked it so much that we went there every day and became friends with the chef, George. George liked us so much that he offered us his secret recipe for real German-style *Rahmgeschnetzeltes* that was passed down to him from his great grandmother. Although George used beef, I make this recipe with venison backstrap and it is superb!

1 to 2 pounds of venison backstrap, cut into small strips
Salt and pepper to taste
6 medium mushrooms, sliced
1 small onion, finely sliced
12 ounces heavy whipping cream
2 medium pickles, finely sliced
2 tomatoes, blanched*, peeled, and diced
Dollop of mustard
Pat of butter

Heat oil in a large skillet over high heat. Add venison strips and sauté for 5 minutes. Add salt and pepper, remove from pan, and keep on a warmed plate. Place mushrooms and onion into the skillet and cook about 3 to 4 minutes. Add cream and let cook for 5 to 7 minutes. Add pickles, tomatoes, mustard, butter, and more salt and pepper if desired. Chef George recommends serving this with rice and a nice salad.

* Slice a cross in tomato tops, place in boiling water for 10 seconds, then immediately put them in cold water. This allows you to peel off the skins.

Stuffed Venison

No matter what amounts you use, you can't mess this recipe up!

1 to 2 pounds venison tenderloins or backstrap,
    pounded to ¼-inch thick or thinly sliced
Dash of salt
½ cup finely chopped fresh basil
    or 1 tablespoon dried basil
1 head garlic, roasted*, casings removed, and smashed
½ cup thinly sliced smoked gouda or goat cheese
    (optional)
2 tablespoons olive oil
¼ cup shallots (if not available use yellow onion)
¼ cup white wine
¼ cup chicken stock
1 tablespoon honey or Dijon mustard
1 tablespoon butter

Preheat oven to 350 degrees.

Sprinkle venison with salt and basil. Spread garlic in center of tenderloin, add cheese, then roll up and secure with kitchen twine or toothpicks. Sear tenderloins on all sides in a large ovenproof skillet with the olive oil over high heat. Place pan in oven and roast for 20 minutes, or until desired doneness (medium-rare is delicious!), being careful not to overcook. Remove meat from pan, cover with foil, and set aside.

Place pan with meat drippings back on stove over medium heat. Add the shallots and sauté until translucent. Add the wine and deglaze the pan. Add the chicken stock and bring to a boil. Reduce heat and stir in the mustard and butter. Pour sauce over venison and serve.

* To roast 1 head of garlic: Cover the garlic with 2 tablespoons olive oil and wrap in foil. Place in oven and bake at 400 degrees for 20 to 30 minutes or until soft. (Can be done ahead of time.)

CHAPTER
5

SACRED VENISON

Awhisper of wet fog hung before me, touchable and delicious. Like a reassuring maternal blanket of security for a child, the drifting gray cloud caressed my face and soul with a mystical embrace twenty-five feet up in the giant, towering oaktree on my sacred swamp's edge. The predawn had come and gone with a slow, subtle change from pitch dark to barely visible. My spirit was on approach towards Runway Number One to the land of the eternal beast, and I settled in for spiritual touchdown. I nudged my face into the cool, damp wind and thrust my tongue like a gnat-snatching lizard, licking the spicy air. It tasted wonderful— almost like Cajun caffeine with the variety of pungent textures and aromas wafting off the black peat cattail marsh below me; a stimulating punch of tastes augmented by the yummy stench of rotting forest floor debris. My spirit soared as if uplifted by the swirling updrafts of life's easy breathing throbbing all around me, a damn orgy of the senses in a silent scream. And yet, I just sat there like a human radar sponge, my spirit dancing naked around a tribal campfire while I remained rock solid still. All at once I was as calm as the still air, but fired up, way up inside a torrent of emotions. No doubt about it. I was bowhunting, and as always, the nothingness was everything and more. I clamored to understand. I closed my eyes and grinned a Cheshire grin, bubbling with energy and dreams. The secret to life is to be alive. To live ultimately by one's own hand and one's independent devices. To hunt. To kill. To eat. To live. To be happy. The bridge of sighs transported me there.

It is not only the bewitching hour of the mornings of my life that so move me, when critters hustle about, returning from a night's feeding and intense nocturnal activity; but an equally pivotal moment in my calendar year as the natural season of harvest brings about a planetary alignment of events too powerful to ignore. There is a mysterious goat's head soup brewing in the air as a swirling concoction of life's blood and guts, testosterone, estrogen, adrenaline, electricity, energy, spirit, attitude, and endorphins flows like a whitewater rapids cocktail. The mind is clear, almost feeling shut down, while at the same time a varied graphic abstract vision erupts involuntarily from time to time piquing the imagination.

With my head resting against the rough yet soothing supportive bark of the ancient tree, I go blank and flatline. I hear in my peripheral senses, the squawking geese and preening mallards off in the distance of the wetlands providing a gentle soundtrack to my blank dream sequence; sound, sight, and thought melt as one with the thick air around me. Damn, I need this shit. Need it bad. I hump the wild to take it all in. There is no baglimit on happiness.

And so broils another heart-expanding dynamo in the wild, a virtual thrill guaranteed every time I go beyond the pale pavement searching for the Great Spirit that seeks me. I know of the convenience of insulation, perceived as protection from the discomfort of her elements, but I virtually crave her extremes head on, Full Bluntal Nugity. There is no wind nor rain nor sleet nor icy snowblo that could possibly deter me from facing her glory up close and personal, face to face with all she offers. I avoid climate-controlled environments for the sheer thump of adventure. Intensely augmented by the challenge to penetrate the beasts' nearly overwhelming defense mechanisms with the demands of the ultra-close-range bow and arrow, you have yourself a full-blown earthly monster of a gitdown. I crave fullblown earthly monsters. I gitdown.

Having dined mostly on the succulent prime flesh of pure venison backstraps my entire adult life, I have come to expect and demand this prime, vital sustenance. I settle for nothing less, and everything else is inferior. My sacred temple deserves only the best. Everything short of ultimate ultimately sucks. I keep my motor clean and strictly run gonzo octane racefuel in this sonofabitch. I purr, therefor I am. Quality of life is a race, and I'm running strong, way out front, coming round the bend at fullspeed, yet missing nary a heart-stroking beautiful sight along the way. Each bump and obstacle is taken in and deeply appreciated for its challenge and diversion. My map is the road less traveled. It's all mine. My hiway stretches before me like a turbulent river of beautiful, smiling, naked women. I redline with glee.

I make my own way. When man decided to hire others to do his dirtywork, he foolishly backed away from life's greatest connection. Cause-and-effect is surely the most important lesson to be had. We are born at point A and we will die at point B. What could be more important than performing our personal life-sustaining functions, hands-on? I say we're too busy accumulating stuff instead of accumulating quality experiences. Living is everything. Everything is living.

The fog is in patches now. A wet slab here, a drifting clump there. Twitting birds are everywhere around me again this morning, bringing with their every chirp that wild vibrancy that is every hunt. I twist my head and gaze to and fro ever so slowly so as not to disrupt this wonderful natural activity that I am a part of. There, from a light-fractured smoke of gray comes a deer's head, its two omniscient radar ears scanning our forest. His presence satisfies me thoroughly, and I am once again moved by his uncanny caution and alertness. But eventually, after much patience and thrill, my fifty-plus seasons' lessons and mistakes guide me to fulldraw, the mystical flight of my arrow ready to complete life's natural cycle. The bloodtrail is but a short one. My lucky arrow left my bow but never really disconnected from my person. My very being rode that shaft straight through the vitals of the beast, transecting its heart and lungs, and like it, I too was coated in blood. Beautiful, red, life-giving blood. In the wind he's still alive. I thank the Great Spirit when I partake in this sacred flesh, now and forever.

Easy Venison Roast

Easy, step-by-step instructions for a main course made the Nuge way. Try this recipe with other big game, too!

1 3- to 4-pound venison roast
2 cups Allegro Game Tame Marinade
2 to 3 cups mixed stewing vegetables, chopped

Place roast in a crock-pot. Pour Game Tame Marinade over roast and cook on low setting for 6 to 8 hours. One hour before meat is done, add chopped vegetables to roast. Enjoy!

Stuffed Venison Roast

1 3-pound venison roast
¼ cup salt
¼ cup baking soda
Water
2 tablespoons salad oil
5 to 10 strips bacon, cut into pieces
1 green pepper, diced
1 small onion, chopped
1 12-ounce package smoked kielbasa, cooked and sliced
Seasoned salt to taste
Dash of garlic powder

Soak roast overnight in the refrigerator in salt, baking soda, and enough water to cover the meat completely. Remove roast from water and discard liquid. Heat salad oil in a saucepan, add bacon, green pepper, onion, and kielbasa, and sauté until vegetables are tender. Sprinkle with seasoned salt.

Cut roast in half and fill with half the kielbasa mixture. Replace top half of roast and spoon remaining mixture over the top. Season with salt and a dash or two of garlic powder. Wrap in aluminum foil, place in a casserole dish and bake at 350 degrees for 2 hours. Remove aluminum foil and consume!

Venison Honey Roast

This is a quick and easy recipe for an impressive meal.

Salt and pepper (optional)
1 2-pound rolled shoulder roast
¼ cup honey
¾ cup brown sugar
¼ cup orange juice
½ cup water

Preheat oven to 350 degrees. Salt and pepper roast, place in a roasting pan, and cook uncovered for 30 minutes. In a small bowl, thoroughly mix the honey, brown sugar, and orange juice. Spread the honey mixture evenly on all sides of the roast saving some of the mixture for basting. To prevent sticking, add ½ cup of water to the pan before returning to oven. Return roast to oven uncovered and cook about 1 hour longer for rare, 1½ hours for medium to well-done. Baste occasionally with the honey mixture during roasting. Serve with garden vegetables. Serves 4 to 6.

Venison Roast with Sour Cream Sauce

⅓ cup cider vinegar
1 cup dry white wine
1 carrot, peeled and diced
1 celery stalk, trimmed and diced
1 onion, peeled and diced
2 tablespoons whole black peppercorns
1 teaspoon whole allspice
1 teaspoon juniper berries
1 teaspoon fresh thyme
3 to 4 bay leaves
Salt and pepper to taste
8 ounces bacon, diced
1 3-pound boneless venison shoulder roast, trimmed of fat
1 cup sour cream at room temperature
3 tablespoons flour
Zest of 1 lemon
1 rounded tablespoon of Dijon mustard
Lemon slices and lingonberries or cranberries for garnish

Combine cider vinegar, white wine, Dijon mustard, carrot, celery, lemon zest, onion, peppercorns, allspice, juniper berries, thyme, and bay leaves in a large casserole dish. Place venison roast in dish, cover with marinade, and refrigerate for 3 to 4 days, turning once each day. Remove meat from marinade, brush off vegetables, and pat dry.

Season meat lightly with salt and pepper.

Sauté bacon in heavy skillet until bacon begins to crisp. Remove bacon with slotted spoon. Place the roast into the hot fat, and sear quickly on all sides. Strain marinade and reserve juices. Remove roast when browned and place in a crock-pot. Quickly sear vegetables in remaining fat to brown lightly and place them in the crock-pot with the roast.

Pour the strained marinade into a small saucepan and cook over high heat until reduced by half, about ⅔ cup. Pour over roast and vegetables. Simmer roast in crock-pot until tender, about 4 hours. (Choose setting according to how long you wish to cook—the lower the setting, the longer the braising will take). Remove roast from juices and keep warm.

In a small bowl, combine the sour cream and flour, add to the juices in the crock-pot, and cook for 15 minutes. Strain the mixture through a fine sieve, pressing the vegetables to extract their juices or place mixture in a blender and blend until very smooth.

Garnish plates with slices of lemon and lingonberries or cranberries. Slice roast and spoon sauce over. Serve with dumplings, spaetzle, or egg noodles. Serves 4 to 6.

Venison Roast with Spices

1 5- to 6-pound venison roast
Salt and pepper to taste
1 teaspoon allspice
1 dozen whole cloves
1 to 2 teaspoons cayenne pepper
½ pound bacon
4 medium onions, diced
2 cups diced celery
2 cups diced carrots
1 cup red wine
1 cup water
2 sticks butter

Rub salt and pepper into roast and sprinkle with allspice, cloves, and cayenne pepper. Wrap bacon around roast and secure with toothpicks. Place roast in roasting pan and surround with onions, celery, red wine, water, and butter. Cover and bake in a 400 degree oven for 1 hour. Spoon pan liquids over the roast, reduce oven to 275 degrees, and simmer until desired doneness.

The secret to life is to be
alive. To live ultimately by
one's own hand and one's
independent devices.
To hunt. To kill. To eat.
To live. To be happy.
There is no baglimit
on happiness.

6

DINNER ON THE HOOF

n the prolonged silence of the deerblind, my ten-year-old son, Rocco, lifted his head from his hands and sighed. With his binoculars, he carefully scanned the long, wide greenfield before us, then shuffled his legs and backed into his oldman's lap. He leaned his head against my shoulder and just kind of snuggled. I grabbed a handful of his shoulder and squeezed back, a broad, exceedingly happy grin overtaking my face. My eyes welled up with powerful, loving paternal emotion, absolutely tickled that we were not just here together, but *intensely* here together. I could not have been more pleased. Even the physical setting took on a special glow. The fading Texas sun was a brilliant fireball blazing through the January winter gray sky behind us, and its fading shine drenched the entire south Texas landscape in that bronze touch so special to the bewitching hour endgame of every hunt. The prickly pear cactus shimmered like green pearls; the purple sage glistened as if it were oiled. On a mesquite limb outside our window, a stunning male cardinal was as bright red as red can be. A Mexican Terra Terra eagle's white head stood out in the graphic tangled sea of Tejas puckerbrush, and you could almost see the shadows move. Time stood still.

At a young age, Rocco has become a real hunter, and for that I'm very proud. His patience again this day was unexpected from such a young boy, and his natural inquisitiveness proved he was genuinely interested and excited about this annual wild outdoor adventure we shared. Sure he spends some time on his electronic gametoys, and it takes serious parental discipline to manage his TV time, but the real point is that we hunt together more and more every year. And when we do, like with his older brother Toby, these joyous and more open and intimate father-and-son-bonding connections that otherwise just don't happen under most day in and day out conditions regularly occur. It's not just pleasant; it's not just fun. I am convinced that it is actually life saving in most instances when a young person discovers his instinctual touch with the Great Spirit and, through her inescapable Tooth, Fang, and Claw reality, all life she provides naturally in the hunting endeavor. It is that powerful. As he sat there in my lap, I gently caressed the back of his head and neck, incredibly relieved that this was happening again. I am driven as his father to guide, nurture, and love him, constantly in preparation for his eventual quest for independence. That's a parent's job last time I checked. We talk each night before bed, do chores together, have great daily reviews at the dinnertable throughout the year, and I make sure we spend as much quality, heart-to-heart time together as possible. How some parents can do any less is a mystery to me. But it is these times afield that really bring out the best in us, and I wouldn't trade them for anything in this world. Many families know this and cultivate it wisely. If only more parents would do the same.

Our heads jerked up in unison, for the sunset glow brought a flash to our eyes as a majestic whitetailed buck edged into the field. The atmosphere in the elevated coop changed dramatically from peace and love to full red predator alert. Slowly we each raised our binoculars for a looksee, and without a word, Rocco cautiously slid his little Remington Sniper .243 from its rack, and eased his fanny from dad's lap onto his own chair. With his tall, wide, trophy nine-point antlers aglow in the magic light, the beautiful mature buck was obviously a shooter. A nod from our friend and Rancho Encantado guide, Mike Hehman, gave the greenlight, and Rocco snugged into the buttstock of the youth-sized rifle. I didn't have to say a word because all our rangetime and hunter safety lessons together were solidly drilled into his head for many years, and he acted like a veteran hunter. Slowly he positioned the rifle into a perfect rest against the back of his chair and against the sandbag on the windowsill. The big buck was 140 yards out and facing away a little too much for a quality shot. Rocco knew to wait for a broadsider in order to precisely place the 70-grain payload into the vitals for a quick death.

I watched intently through my binos and was much more nervous than my son. At the precise moment that the buck turned broadside, Rocco's index finger snicked off the safety and I heard him take a deep breath. Halfway through his exhale the stainless barrel bucked with a loud bang, and the buck kicked hard and made a mad dash deathrun straight for us. Shot clean through the heart, the buck only made it halfway before piling up stonedead without a twitch. Like tres hombres, in unison the three of us let out a rejoiceful YEEEHAA! and swapped hi-fives all around. I was giddy, Rocco was proud, and Mike was impressed. The deer was dead.

Through his Leica scope, Rocco covered the deer with a chambered round for a moment, but it was clear he was finished. Emptying the rifle, we tried to calm down as we descended the tower's ladder, approaching the magnificent beast with awe, joy, appreciation, and respect. Sure enough, the bullet hole confirmed the marksmanship mastery of First Sergeant Sniper Force One Rocco Winchester Nuge, and we sat there stroking and admiring the spectacular specimen of the world's favorite animal. Mike field-aged the buck at six-and-a-half years, and a roll of film was exposed in the last of the big day's light. It was mystical. It was perfect.

With a special bounce in his step and fire in his heart, Rocco retold the story to our fellow hunters back at camp. Because Texas is smart enough to have no minimum age requirement for young hunters, Rocco and other boys and girls have the opportunity to experience this dynamic hunting lifestyle with their families at an age when the alternatives can surely steer kids down undesirable and dangerous paths. We always say, "If you take your kids hunting, you won't have to hunt for your kids." Amen and pass the smiles . . . and the chow! 𐐝

Stuffed, Rolled Venison Log

2 pounds ground venison
1 medium onion, chopped fine
1½ cups Quaker oats
Salt and pepper to taste
4 tablespoons A-1 sauce
8 slices boiled ham
1 pound shredded mozzarella cheese

Mix venison, onion, oats, salt and pepper, and A-1 sauce in a large bowl and shape into a meat loaf. Lay heavy foil on a flat surface, place meat loaf in center of foil, and flatten out to 12 x 14 inches and ½-inch thick. Lay ham on top of meat loaf side by side to cover loaf. Sprinkle on cheese. Roll into log. Ham and cheese should be in center. Pinch end of loaf so cheese won't leak out.

Place in baking dish, cover with foil, and bake at 350 degrees for 1 hour. Remove foil and let brown for 30 minutes.

Italian Venison Casserole

1 teaspoon venison seasoning
2 pounds ground venison
2 cups elbow macaroni, uncooked
2 tablespoons margarine or butter
1 cup chopped onion
2 cups tomato sauce
1½ cups tomato paste
1 tablespoon Italian seasoning
8 ounces mozzarella or pizza cheese

Preheat oven to 350 degrees. Mix venison seasoning with ground venison and let stand for 15 minutes. Meanwhile, cook elbow macaroni according to package directions and drain. Melt the butter or margarine in a skillet and brown the ground venison and onion. Combine the venison mixture with the macaroni, tomato sauce, tomato paste, and Italian seasoning in a large casserole dish. Sprinkle cheese over the top and bake until the top is golden brown. Excellent served with salad and garlic toast.

Swedish Meatballs with Venison
by Shemane

This venison meatball dish is a lifesaver for those last minute occasions when you suddenly discover that guests are coming for dinner and you need a quick yet tasty recipe—and you want it to look as though you spent hours in the kitchen. This recipe is so good that my 100-percent-Norwegian grandmother can't tell I use wild game.

1 to 2 pounds ground venison
¼ cup heavy cream
½ cup dry seasoned bread crumbs
½ teaspoon salt
½ teaspoon pepper
1 egg
1 small onion, chopped
Sprinkle of parsley
¼ teaspoon allspice
¼ teaspoon nutmeg
2 cans cream of mushroom soup or cream of chicken
   and mushroom soup
Wide noodles

Preheat oven to 400 degrees. Spray medium glass baking dish with nonstick spray.

Swedish Meatballs with Venison (continued)

Mix all ingredients except for soup and noodles in a large mixing bowl. Pour into baking dish and mash.

Using a spatula, cut horizontal and vertical lines that leave 1- to 2-inch pieces of mixture. (Don't worry that the meat will not completely separate. The meatballs won't be completely round, but you'll dazzle your guests with the mouthwatering meal.) Place in oven and cook for 20 to 25 minutes.

Cook noodles in water according to package directions.

In a large sauté pan, warm soup and stir thoroughly. Remove meatballs from oven and spoon into the soup mixture, further separating the pieces. Mix and serve over the hot noodles. Serves 4 to 6.

Jamaican Jerk Venison

This is one tasty and different way to fuse North American and Caribbean cuisines. This is my favorite Jamaican Jerk recipe, which I recently used with venison to great applause. This recipe goes well with fish, yard bird, and beef, too; and the "heat" can be adjusted for your guests.

6 scallions, green only, thinly sliced
2 large shallots, finely minced
2 large cloves of garlic, finely minced
1 tablespoon finely minced fresh ginger
1 tablespoon seeded, ribbed, and finely minced
    Scotch Bonnet pepper
1 tablespoon ground allspice
1 teaspoon ground black pepper
¼ teaspoon cayenne pepper
1 teaspoon ground cinnamon
½ teaspoon ground nutmeg
1 tablespoon fresh thyme leaves or 1 teaspoon
    dried thyme
1 tablespoon dark-brown sugar
Dash of salt
½ cup fresh orange juice
½ cup rice vinegar
¼ cup red-wine vinegar
¼ cup soy sauce
¼ cup olive oil
2 to 4 pounds venison

Jamaican Jerk Venison (continued)

In a medium bowl, combine scallions, shallots, garlic, ginger, and Scotch Bonnet pepper. In a separate bowl, combine the allspice, black pepper, cayenne, cinnamon, nutmeg, thyme, dark-brown sugar, and salt, and mix thoroughly. Whisk in the orange juice, vinegars, and soy sauce. Slowly drizzle in the oil, whisking constantly. Add the scallion mixture and stir to combine. Let rest at least 1 hour. Wash meat well, pat dry, and place in a large bowl. Add the sauce and rub into the meat on all sides. Cover and refrigerate overnight.

Preheat oven to 350 degrees. Move marinated meat to a shallow roasting pan.

Prebake for 45 minutes, turning and basting occasionally.

Prepare hot coals for grilling. Grill meat over medium heat for 25 to 30 minutes, turning 4 or 5 times, and dabbing with remaining marinade.

We always say, "If you take your kids hunting, you won't have to hunt for your kids." Amen and pass the smiles . . . and the chow!

7

ROCK 'N' ROLL HOGMANDO

With fire in my eyes and an everpresent tasty wisp of prehistoric foam bubbling at the corners of my mouth, I have madly and gleefully chased packs of wildly bellering hounds over hill and dale, up ridiculous vine-gripped mountainsides, and through the nastiest, puckerbrushed, fleshripping, briar-infested hellhole muckzonia swamps a sane whiteman dare not tread. The harder the run, the quicker the foam takes on a handsome cherry swirl appearance I'm told.

I love the fullthrottled adrenaline pumping hot pursuit of bear, lions, coons, housecats, escaped chimps, small children, scared women, and everything else that can be legally chased and/or hunted. But the ultimate rock 'n' roll hellraiser for me is when there is some stinking, godawful putrid, tantalizingly pissed-off, mud-encrusted, musk-saturated, urine-infested, fuming swine, snapping ivory and hauling nonkosher ass ahead of the hungry spirithounds, to bring out the best natural born killer God ever created in all of us. Where I come from hot houndsbreath is a spice. And wild pigs are just plain cool as hell. I love to watch em, hunt em, fight em, kill em, nut em, stab em, shoot em, slap em, gut em, bite em, eat em, know em, give em the finger, and dance naked with em before, during, and after the BBQ. When it's time to have some good, clean, all-American legal fun and games, bring on the cross-country porkchop slammajamboree. It's like a country and western concert without the bad music. Gotta luv that. Though a rabble-rousing hotleg run with a pack of God's best designed fire-eyed, chainbustin', snortmaster trail-blazing howlers is my favorite method of snagging BBQ pork on the hoof. I get an absolute kick out of every pigkillin' maneuver you can possibly think of. I luv em, run em, stalk em, kick em, wrestle em, slap em, bait em, trap em, call em, yell at em, corner em, jump em, ambush em, and surprize em backstage at the Grand Old Opry. I love hog hunting so much that I have created my own hunting operation at home so I can have my own wild porkfun any old time I wanna. Godbless America and pass the hot sauce!

At my Sunrize Acres HuntRanch in Michigan, I have the most beautiful pure Austrian, longhaired, kranky, rock 'n' roll, bent attitude wild boars you have ever laid eyes on—or a knife or a bullet or arrow into. With long, coarse hair in black, brown, red, gold, silver, calico, brindle, and varying combinations and shades of all of the above, accented with spectacular razor-sharp ivory jutting out of their prehistoric lips, and a disposition that only me, their mothers, and God could love, these huge, ornery beasts are just what the good BBQ doctor ordered for a weary old rock 'n' roll guitarboy to cleanse the soul and humble the heart. Besides feeding my family with the best damn healthy, pure organic, other white flesh known to man, the hunt provides equal protein for the soul. If nature heals, pork exhilarates.

So there I was, back in the porkchop wild again feeling wild and free, hungry and alive. Perfect as perfect can be. I had my trusty bow and arrows tuned up, Nugent Blade broadheads as razorsharp as my hunter's mindset and as physically and psychologically cocked, locked, and ready to rock, doc, ultraprimed for some serious hands-on beast harvesting. My mind was right and I was in full kill mode. The sky was dark and the air was cool, and I had just scared over two million unsuspecting civilians on the not-so-mean streets of America as I wrapped up my five thousandth rockout concert, including 133 in the last seven months with KISS, on the number one rocktour in the freeworld for the year 2000. I was both beat to a pulp and powered up for the best hunting season of my greazy fifty-three years, as I settled into the towering white oak treestand on my favorite ridge in Nugent Forest. Ahhhhh!

I couldn't drag my wounded rock 'n' roll ass outta bed early this first day home from the long tour, but the wind called my name, and I heard her loud and clear as the ideal southwest wind set me up for an afternoon ambush. If the sounder of handsome hogs I had seen recently repeated their acorn orgy schedule, I would be porkbound with the hammerdown in a short while. With my Rutherford safety harness snuggly attached around my shoulders, butt, and hips, I nocked a 500-grain carbon arrow and put on my Primos Mossy Oak camo facemask with almost cocky confidence. I had experienced many a day afield on my sacred Sunrize huntgrounds without getting a shot at anything, but I always seem to believe I will. This day I felt it powerfully.

Maybe it was the ever-darkening hunter's sky overhead, accented by the always stimulating, beautiful birdlife all about. Maybe it was the long overdue, intensely anticipated first bowhunt of the fall, or maybe I'm just stupid, but my grinning face and laughing heart could not be denied. I'm hunting, baby, and nothing else matters! Rooted deeply within the always wonderfully positive metaphysical power of the hunt, you couldn't convince me that anything like Janet Reno even existed. Even the oldest, scarred boars looked good compared to Mr. Reno. Everything was much too nice. I say YOWZA YOWZA and pass the spirit! Fully erect, if you please.

A squadron of flitting, chirping robins staged above me in the leafy treetops, squawking and divebombing with Tora Tora excitement as the driving instinct to prepare for their annual migration took over. I felt it and joined in as best I could, smiling even more now, knowing how connected I was with them here at my natural buoyant predator position way up high. They eat worms, I eat pork. Beautiful. My kosher friends notwithstanding, pigmeat is grand, natural, ultrayummy chow, and my desire to feed it to my family kicked my hunter's heart into overdrive as a branch snapped in the distance directly behind me. My ESP-hearing amplifiers made up for the forty-some-odd years (and I do mean odd) of outrageous sonic bombast rock 'n' roll decibel overload abuse, and I turned ultraslowly to have a looksee. Through my ever-handy Leupold binos, I could see dark, animated forms down the tangled ravine, due south about 75 yards away, in and out of the thick stuff. Oh yeah! A pork parade comin' my way! A grunting, huffing undertow resonated in the depths of the big timber. How lovely.

The sturdy API ladderstand was quiet enuf for me to turn hard left, positioning me for a possible arrowshot if they continued on their current path. For a while they did, but before they cut the distance in half, the big black lead beast led them away from me to the east, and I had to squirm silently around the tree the other way. Much to my surprize, when I turned left, there was a huge gray, silvery old boar directly under my perch, rooting and gobbling up the sweet white acorns that were scattered across the September forest floor. His huge head jerked up on point and alert as I froze in midspin, hoping I didn't blow it. After a momentary pause, the swine couldn't resist the succulent mast all around him and returned to pigging out. Ever so cautiously I tried to get on him, but by the time I got straightened out he was too far right and I could not get the bow thataway. Had he been the only hog there, I suppose I could have stood up and pivoted hard for a shot, but lo and behold, an even bigger, mud-encrusted black boar was bringing up the rear, about to enter my ideal shotzone to the left as he too fed on the ultimate acorn bait.

God baits. Go figure.

The moment really made me appreciate the extra effort I invest each spring, fertilizing my white oak groves in these family woods. Typically oaks only produce acorns every other year or so, but since I began with my simple triple-19 fertilizing efforts, we get a great crop every year, and the deer, turkeys, squirrels, grouse, wood ducks, mallards, and hogs go wild for them. So do I! And it looked like I was about to get me some acornfed pork if I played my hunter's cards right. Blackjack!

I held my breath as the big boy snorted and grunted amongst the colored leaves and forest debris, vacuuming protein from Ma

Nature's pantry below. I gracefully swung my upright bow along with his movements, and as he stopped to root a spot, I came to fulldraw and began my ritualistic bowhunter's prayer. My eyes and my pointing arrow were one with his forward ribcage, a third of the way up from his bellyline behind his foreleg and shoulder, and as I kissed my release trigger and finished ". . . and of the Holy Spirit of the Wild, Amen," my shoulder muscles pulled tight and my arrow zinged across the 30 yards square into the muddy hair I was looking at with a solid THUMPH, in and out of his tough, rugged torso in an instant. With a Courtney Love-like squeal and a jump, he scrambled wildly around the wooded rize, as the previously all white, now all red, arrow stuck into the ground beyond him. Other hogs erupted behind me with a clamor and a chorus of grunting swinespeak, but my shishkebabed hairy porkchop express slammed head-on into a giant maple tree with a terminal whack, and he kicked his last all within 35 yards and three seconds. POA (pork on arrival). The other whitemeat has landed. Shopping with Ted. Always an adventure. Always good food. It's so damned pure I feel like Mother Theresa with a sharp stick.

I watched the other gorgeous Austrian hogs mill about in piglike confusion, much like a throng of stoned, lost Grateful Dead fans, till they melted away into the dark forest beyond. I breathed a happy sigh of relief and looked to the now burning red and orange sunsetting heavens in solemn thanx to the good Lord for this awesome system of sustain yield Tooth, Fang, and Claw truth. How cool is this?

The 300-pound truck of a pig was so damn ugly he was beautiful. Though he hadn't actually torched any children that I knew of, we called him Janet anyway. The resemblance was frightening. The only thing missing was the purple dress and he-man haircut. Long, gnarly calico boarhair graced his muddy gray warrior head, snout, and torso. Nearly four inches of sharp-edged fighting ivory sabers protruded from his mean-looking porcine lips. Rips and gouges and scars adorned his entire warrior bulk, and he was a joy to look at. I exposed a roll of film on the stunning beast, gutted him, and dragged him into a clearing drenched in the last glow of the day. Magictime for nature lovers everywhere.

From the expert butchering shop of Joe Nagle in Homer, Michigan, Janet's organic flesh produced the finest breakfast sausage that Bob Evans or Jimmy Dean could ever dream of, and I relive the moving encounter any old time I close my eyes and remember. No wonder I don't watch TV. Compared to this dynamic thrill, it all sucks.

Wild Boar Chops

Only a few campers are fortunate enough to enjoy this delicious game meat—the rest must be content with domestic pork chops. But if you should bag a wild boar, serve it this way.

4 wild boar chops
Salt and pepper to taste
Flour for dredging
3 tablespoons fat from boar
Dash of paprika
24 raisins
2 pounds apples, cored (but not peeled) and cut into
    thick slices
2 tablespoons brown sugar
¼ cup hot water

Sprinkle chops with salt, pepper, and flour and brown well on both sides in a large skillet heated with the oil. Sprinkle chops with paprika, place 6 raisins on top of each browned chop, and cover with apple slices, brown sugar, and ¼ cup of hot water. Cover skillet and simmer until well done, about 40 minutes. Serves 2 to 4 (1 large or 2 small chops per person).

Marinade for Wild Boar Chops

This marinade can also be used for beef.

¾ cup soy sauce
½ cup oil
1 teaspoon mustard powder
1 tablespoon ginger
½ teaspoon Accent seasoning

Mix all ingredients, pour over chops, and marinate overnight or 7 to 8 hours, turning several times.

8

TEXAS WILD BOAR BBQ

My poor, pathetic, overly abused, sore rock 'n' roll bones were screaming in terror for relief, begging for mercy, but I crawled outta bed anyway. More than one hundred torturous, ultrafun nights of all-American rock 'n' roll hell just came to a crashing, glowrious close, and the remnants of my guitar and psyche were put to rest in their annual autumn hibernation coffin. I smiled and made little wounded varmint noises under my breath as I dragged my weary beaten hulk from the warm, snuggly bed and into the bathroom of our hunter's lodge. I rubbed my eyes and stretched slowly and long, begging my predator being within to rise up again for the soul-stirring annual ritual of the sacred hunt. I coughed and wheezed, sniffled and stumbled into the dark bathroom to prime my spiritual pump, and, little by little, the spirit came to life as visions of great Texas critters danced before my dreamy mind's eye. It's hunting season, baby, and nothing can stop me now! Say YOWZA and pass the attitude!

Just the night before, I had whipped myself, my band, and five thousand hearty Abilenian BloodBrothers into a frothy patriotic frenzy with a rousing two-hour rockout. With blazing fire in his eyes, one pissed-off, testosterone-infested Great White Buffalo stampeded across the prairies of our souls as an electric bonfire erupted all around with an incendiary rendition of "The Star Spangled Banner." There wasn't a dry eye or unclenched fist in the house just a few hours ago, and now I was just trying to keep my eyes open. Game and ranch manager Randy Rifenburgh lovingly brought me a hot cup of java out of sheer pity, and I joined friends Ronnie and Gary to take on a wonderful, cold, dewy wet Texas sunrise adventure, bow and arrows in hand.

This massive chunk of Texas real estate near Abilene was coming to life a little better than I was, but immediately the adrenaline caffeine of the wild charged me up with a new vitality and aliveness. The broomweed and mesquite were an uncharacteristic bright green even in the predawn shimmer. Gorgeous splashes of brilliant purple, reds, yellows, and some white and blue augmented the rich, lush vegetation rolling up and down the stunning landscape, beautiful eye candy inspiration for a tired old rockdog. The ample rains of late summer had turned a drought-stricken moonscape into a sea of graphic beauty. The red, maroon, and purple prickly pear cactus blooms were glimmering everywhere, and flitting golden monarch butterflies fluttered atop the waves of color on their timeless migration through Texas. I took another swig of hot coffee, gazed across the expanse, and clutched my bowgrip a little tighter. I hung on as the pickup truck negotiated the rocky, broken baja ground. We twisted and bumped and grinded our way up, up, and over one ridge after another, and finally came to a stop where the gray and blue sky met a shiny green treeline. Randy showed me the gametrail cutting the tangle of Spanish daggers and mesquite brush where he had constructed a nifty groundblind facing the morning updrafts and shadows. A Sweeney cornfeeder was positioned in the thick stuff below us, and I was told that, as a result of much scouting and preparation, a number of huge old boar hogs were seen crossing this ridge on some mornings. Now I was awake, as I could sense—actually smell and taste—the pungent wild around me. A little bird of prey whispered in my ear, "Nuge, we have decompression. You will be alright now!"

Hogs, kids! We're in hog country! I absolutely love hunting for hogs. And in the strange vaportrail that is a long, rock 'n' roll tour aftermath, I needed me some big hog hunting medicine right about now to help me unwind. Rocketfuel for life. I need it bad!

With his *Spirit of the Wild* vidcam on his shoulder, Ronnie took his perch on the stool at the rear of the coop behind me, and I gathered myself into a comfortable shooting position and nocked my arrow. Styled after Mark Mueller's famous shoot-through InvisiBlind, Randy had crafted a large comfortable two-man coop with a dandy three-foot square shooting port up front. This ideal shooting window was covered with a thin veil of camo netting that the archer actually shoots right through. It gave optimum visibility of everything before us while concealing us in the dark interior from the ultradefense radar eyes of the wildlife.

And wildlife there was. At first light, mourning doves zinged across the horizon by the hundreds, divebombing in and out of the scrub before us in a nonstop aerial dogfight-like frenzy. Bobwhite quail picked and bobbed as they marched along the gravely brush-choked terrain. A Cooper's hawk almost nailed a songbird in an explosion of feathers and splash of dew in a tangle of mesquite brush. I could see a wad of Rio Grande turkeys ducking and weaving as they came and went down in the distant valley, piercing golden sunrays glistening off their iridescent plumage. A flash of orange riveted my attention on a clump of vegetation as a handsome whitetailed buck followed his bright antlers into a small opening. Now my heart really raced, and it wasn't even deer season yet. There were more butterflies maneuvering all around us now. Good Lord, is there anything more beautiful than a Texas sunrise?

But of course there is! A Texas sunrise with huge, nasty, wild boar close by. And even with my old crusty rock 'n' roll ears, thanks to my Walker's Game Ear, I heard a slight crunch of gravel behind us. A combination of clean clothes, the scent containment of the four walls around us, judicious application of Essence of Fall spray from Nature's Essence, and a little hunter's luck, caused whatever was pushing rock nearby not to smell us. It stayed on course, and was getting closer. Come on baby!

With a deep snort and a defiant grunt, his big black snout first showed on the trail to our immediate left, stabbing and rooting the ground. I knew instinctively that Ronnie was rolling amazing *Spirit of the Wild* footage, and I went into predator autopilot as the black and golden beast's intimidating head and massive hulk slowly became visible, inch by inch, grunt by grunt, at a short, hair-raising 10 yards. The sonic bombast outrage and rock 'n' roll frenzy of more than five thousand concerts was nonexistent now as I slowly lifted my bow into shooting position. I was more like a silent eagle than a crazed rock guitar maniac. All those mezmerizing forces that just moments ago defined me, were now completely gone. All I was aware of was the gnarly, heaving chest of coarse hair before my arrowhead, especially the front rib behind his armor-like shoulder blade that housed his pump-station. Nothing else existed. I kissed my right hand fingertips that held my bowstring into the corner of my mouth, and I silently uttered my traditional preshot prayer for the mystical flight of my arrow. Mt. St. Helens was silent just before she blew, too.

My white arrow was gone in a flash, and so was the beast. Where he had stood only a nanosecond before, a small cloud of dust parachuted back to earth with rays of brilliant sunlight cutting in every direction. It was almost crystalline in its shimmer and glow. Like that display, my heartbeat drifted back to a manageable level, the threat of cardiac arrest subsiding. I whooshed a big gulp of air out of my lungs, feeling pretty good about the place my white feathers held on the side of the big wild pig as he exploded out of sight. I looked at Ronnie and into his camera lens and smirked a smart-ass statement about dangerous wild boar and razor-sharp Nugent Blade broadheads. I always get real giddy after the shot. Every arrow I release is very important to me. Very important. A good arrow elates me, a bad one destroys me. I'm a lot of fun to be around when I make a good shot. I'm a pain in the ass otherwise.

It is truly amazing how many hours, days, years, and intense efforts go into the hunt, yet the moment of truth is but a blink of an eye. The killing of game, though powerfully rewarding in protein and thrills, represents maybe a single second in an experience that cannot be measured in time. For every moment of killing, I experience thousands of hours of wonderment and happiness celebrating all those special activities that make the hunting life so exciting. Maybe that's one of the reasons a hunting family feels so much better connected to the precious food that feeds us at our dinnertables. We cannot deny the procedure by which we are sustained, and a deep reverence develops that is mostly lost on assembly line consumers. Damn shame really.

And dine we shall! The 150-pound boar made it only seventy-five yards from our blind, dead in a matter of a few seconds at best. We took some photos to celebrate our hunt, and then tied a Glenn's Deer Handle around his toothy snout for a short drag to the trail where we loaded him up and took him to the cooler to be butchered into family-sized portions. Wild boar pork may very well the ultimate BBQ on the planet—tonight it's javelina for everybody!

Bar-B-Que Sauce for Javelina (Good for All Piggage)

Tomato sauce (lots!)
Brown sugar
Vinegar
Garlic
Onion bits
Pineapple juice
Lemon juice
Prickly pear fruit juice

Combine ingredients in amounts to your own taste. Mix thoroughly, place in a sauce pan, and simmer until heated through. Brush onto javelina meat and bar-b-que.

CHAPTER
9

SNOWHOGS

Damn! It was cold. It was so cold that the fresh snow was so solidly frozen it had the consistency of tiny, dairy, Styrofoam beads. Fortunately and surprizingly, nothing crunched, and it made for silent stalking as I slowly pussyfooted my way through the icy, breathtaking winter woods. SnoBoy with bow was in search of beasto McPorksicle; old hairtooth WildBoar McSnort of the frozen wilds, his bad self, as pretty as ugly can be.

My sacred deerseason in Michigan had finally come to a thrilling and always heart-wrenching close for yet another glowrious fall and winter of dream hunting. But now the real fun begins—chasing amazing wild hogs through the deeper winter months. Extremely harsh, even dangerous conditions scare some guys out of the woods, but with an adequately bold predator attitude and the ever changing and developing clothing technology, there is no such thing as too cold for the modern hunter.

My Browning polar fleece snowcamo was good and warm and made me blend invisibly with my winter, water wonderland surroundings. I not only felt as one with nature, I even looked it. Omaha's Carol Davis longjons and LaCrosse Arctic footwear insulated me completely from the bonefreezing ten-below-zero windswept hell-frio. I was so snug in my quality hunting clothing, the only danger for me was getting sweaty if I moved too fast. Nanuck of the Great North wishes!

Proper stalking is 95 percent looking and 5 percent cautious moving. All movement must be accomplished with ultrapredator-like stealth, for all prey animals, even the lowly ugly/handsome swine, are geared for full flight survival escape capabilities. I have learned over the many years of trial and error that a foot hunter cannot possibly move too slowly when stillhunting or stalking. It is imperative that the hunter identify his prey before the quarry senses a predator presence. The nearly impenetrable radar of ears, eyes, and nose of all game species is augmented with an unidentifiable yet mystical network of sensory perception that truly boggles the human mind. If I hear one more citykid call wildlife "defenseless," I think I'm gonna puke! All the defenseless critters are dead and gone and found on your grocer's shelves. The rest of em are still getting away 90 percent of the time. That's why we call it hunting. So be it.

With judicious binocular work, my eyes gobbled up every inch of terrain all around me. I had a slight advantage in that the snowy white topography should cause your average dark-colored wild boar to stand out against the dramatic background. But I dared not rely on that presumption, for I had seen huge black beasts appear seemingly out of nowhere more times than not without a hint of adequate hiding cover to be found. Game is like that. Even a pitch-black hog has enough various shades, textures, and hues to help him disappear in average habitat. What the snow really provided was an advantage for me, the predator. Completely dressed head to toe in broken white camo, I had a wild hair of advantage in pursuit of wild pig with their somewhat less than perfect eyesight. Though hogs can see the slightest movement, their overall vision is not as inescapable as that of their brother the deer or elk. Slow and easy was my best trick.

Slow and easy is not just the best approach for getting in arrow range of game, but ultimately the best lick for optimizing the overall outdoor experience. As one pauses between careful steps, an amazing array of observations become apparent and fill the mind, heart, and soul with powerful spirit-cleansing beauty and joy. The slower and fewer my steps, the more I see, hear, and feel, and ultimately celebrate. So every conscientious step of the hunt provides a smorgasbord of sensual stimuli and lessons of the wild that increase our level of respect and sense of duty to the Spirit of the Wild. My spirit cup runneth over every time I leave the pavement.

This day, like every moving day afield, brought dynamic encounters of the wild kind at every turn. As I paused in a deep ravine surrounded by the most beautiful snow-covered world you could ever dream of, a trio of crows came overhead out of nowhere, screaming and cawing up a storm as they divebombed their archenemy, Mr. Predator, the red-tailed hawk. Mr. TuffGuy Hawk seemed to take great joy in aggravating the black-winged rats, as he sat poised in the branches above, calm and cocky as can be while the crows carried on furiously. I wondered if the crows ever really attacked or hurt a hawk. I have watched them for years and all the crows ever do is fly about madly, raising hell but never actually getting close. It's wild and fascinating.

While all this was going on, a fat bushytailed fox squirrel, oblivious to my invisible presence, hopped and scurried within a few feet of my position, digging intently into the deep snow looking for last fall's acorn stash. He probed about all around me for a long time before ambling off into the towering white oak grove up the ridge and out of sight. On most occasions when I am bowhunting big game, I will take advantage of these close encounters with other legal game to arrow one for the pot, but this time, for unknown reasons, I just watched the little booger make his way thru the snow.

And a good call it was, for the little limbrat had barely disappeared up the trunk of a distant oak when I picked up a slight grunt to my south. Slowly elevating my Leupold binoculars to my eyes, I focused into the tangle of multiflora rose thickets fifty yards behind me and there he was, Sir Tuskerdo McPork!

My bone-numbing, patient, standing-still for so long in frozen silence, appreciating the wild around me with my well-tuned predator radar, had paid off again. From a slight depression in the series of timbered ridges came the unmistakable prehistoric hoary shape of one hell of a gorgeous Austrian boar. With the wind crossing away from him and my Browning snocamo doing its job of concealment, the old toothy Lord of the Swamp ambled slowly in my direction, rooting noisily as he aggressively power-tilled the frozen ground, desperate for winterlocked remnant feed. The crows abruptly ceased their caterwauling and silently winged off into the hinterland beyond the giant trees as I slowly extracted an arrow from my bowquiver. Without taking my eyes off the approaching beast, my arrow found its nock onto my bowstring as if with a mind of its own and my predator mind's eye scanned the world for porcine vitals. I breathed heavily now. We appeared on a perfect collision course, but I had seen this before without getting a shot. I readied myself intensely.

He came on slowly, a beastly grunt per step to further antagonize my psyche. I always say a short Prayer for the Wildthings as I prepare to draw my bow, but I could feel the pressure building as he entered the dangerzone, so I took a deep breath and said an advance prayer now. He came. Ultraslowly I lifted my bow and stared a hole into his chest. The Great Spirit's hand came from above, guiding the beautiful boar's head behind a single stump at 25 yards, covering his radar eyeballs, and my bow made the final elevation inline with his Mack Truck shoulder. I was one with the wind. There was no world outside my tractorbeam vision to his heart. The planets aligned and time stood still as the fully drawn arrow snugged tightly into the corner of my mouth, a primal scream within, and I finished my hunter's prayer. In this totally snow covered place, the heavy white insulation helped my Sims equipped bow discharge with nary a sound, the slice-punch of the razorsharp Nugent Blade against muscled flesh the only sound in the wild, punctuated with the most wonderful deep, guttural, beastly squeal you could ever imagine. In a dreamlike slomotion explosion, the giant hog spun violently, the white feathers of the 500-grain projectile now against his massive shoulder; blood showing instantly as he slammed into the old oak stump, regained his footing, and snorted madly off into the winter wonderland from whence he came. Whew! Can I breathe now?

I knew the shot was real good, and I felt a powerful tingling sensation all over. I have bowkilled many magnificent big game animals in my lifetime, but each and every encounter and occurrence is truly moving. It takes a while to regain my composure. This killing game for the dinnertable is serious stuff, and I, for one, will never let its impact be diminished. I stood there for a few moments, smiling and shaking, and actually chuckling a little laugh. I had done it. Luck had put me in this ravine, the Great Spirit had brought us together, and my lifetime of hunting and archery discipline had brought the goodluck to its proper and ultimately gratifying conclusion. I wiped my nose with the back of my sleeve and let out a whoosh of visible breath, clenched my fist, and audibly exalted a proud predator "YOWZA!" from my guts. My body began to relax.

I strolled over to the tattered stump, now covered on the south side with blood and hair. I knelt down and examined the evidence all around. A single set of parallel tracks meandered to this place, where his explosive departure tore up the ground like a bomb had gone off. The virgin snowfield now had a beautiful abstract artwork of splashed red sprayed along the bulldozed trail to the southeast, not unlike, but much more impressive than, some postmodern artwork in a New York City gallery. And I could smell this sensually stimulating dynamo nature art. The pungent aroma of musky pigstench accented with blood on the snow and fresh rotted oakstump torn asunder was an orgy for the senses. I slumped to the ground and actually sniffed the shrapnel of brown, yellow, gray, red, and black around me. God, it was grand. I sat there taking it all in.

The bloodtrail was a graphic Five Star crimson on white beauty, taking me further yet into the wonderment of a natural winter predator's postcard dream. I took my good old time, pausing to snack on a Three Musketeer candybar and a sip of hi-protein juice from my waterbottle. It was like a damn Spiritual picnic. The crows called again in the distance. There seemed to be a nuthatch or a downy woodpecker on every tree, hammering away and making their cute little squawking songs. I crossed a scramble of turkey tracks at the bottom of the gully, and deer prints were here and there where a small herd of maybe a dozen or so had moved through the oaks earlier this morning. I could see the telltale spoor of a lone coyote that had followed its hopeful meal a ways, then where he cut off for easier and smaller pickings. My smile grew exponentially with each sensually invigorating step and dynamic soul expanding moment.

I nearly stepped on my giant hog as I moved around a clump of snow, for he had died in midstep after a hundred yard flight. The arrow was still in him, sticking out both sides of his barrel-like chest, having taken out both lungs and the main ventricles to his pumpstation. I had provided the beast the most efficient death to be had in the wild. He wasn't badgered and haggled to death nor eaten alive by a canine predator. He wasn't torn to shreds by another wild boar in a fight for dominance, territory, or breeding rights. He didn't contract a deadly disease and suffer a prolonged death. He didn't grow old and get chewed on by a pack of feral dogs. The gorgeous animal had not been tamed, controlled, and caged all his life to be zapped for the canned ham industry in order to provide for someone's Easter dinner. He had simply been killed cleanly, naturally, in the wild where he lived like a wild animal as God had designed him, brought to bag, full cycle, by my well-placed, razorsharp arrow. He suffered none whatsoever, and bled to death painlessly in seconds. I was proud to be an active, reasoning predator.

I knelt at his side, stroked his prehistoric, gnarled course hair, examined his saber-like tusks, and held his magnificent, heavy, handsome beasto head in my hands. With all I had within me, I absorbed the wonderment, anticipation, anxiety, hope, tension, excitement, fear, joy, respect, sights, sounds, smells, thrills, challenge, beauty, stimuli, participation, and food that his very being had provided me.

Throughout my sacred ritual of forever imagining, preparing, dreaming, hunting, stalking, tracking, shooting, sensing, killing, trailing, looking, touching, remembering, photographing, gutting, dragging, loading, hanging, skinning, butchering, wrapping, bar-b-q-ing, seasoning, eating, and the ongoing, never-ending reminiscing of all these magical, mystical predator experiences, my soul soared higher and higher. The spiciness of the delicious, nutritional pork dinner enjoyed by Tribe Nuge as a result of this hunting was outdone only by the spiritual twang of the powerful memories taken deep into my consciousness from every outing. These sensations raged and flowed on like a whitewater torrent of emotions in my mind as I pulled the steaming carcass behind me on a grizzled hair sled through the moonlit sparkling, mesmerizing white snowfield to my waiting truck. I caught myself short as I paused to breathe it all in, and there in the pure whiteness, my shadow walked beside me as if an ancient, skulking ancestor accompanied me on this eternal quest for fire. He does. It's me. 🏹

Boar Roast

A good side dish for the boar roast is stuffed potatoes or cinnamon apples.

1 3½- to 4-pound boar roast
1½ teaspoons dried basil
½ teaspoon pepper
1½ teaspoons ground thyme
3 cloves garlic, smashed
Dash of paprika
4 strips bacon

Remove as much fat as possible from boar roast. Combine basil, pepper, thyme, and garlic and rub into roast on all sides. Sprinkle with paprika and place strips of bacon across top of roast. Place roast in a roasting bag and follow the bag instructions for roast pork. Roast until well-done—about 3 to 4 hours. (Cooking time is determined by the size and shape of roast. For large roasts, use a meat thermometer. Pork must be cooked to an internal temperature of 160 degrees. Pork ordered well-done should be cooked to an internal temperature of 170 degrees.)

CHAPTER 10

I LIKE MY PORK PISSED OFF

So we have a huge, dead pig before us, do we? How beautiful is that! Every stirring, exciting, stimulating moment of the hunt remains vivid in our mindseye, heart, and soul forever if we have followed our proper, reasoning predator conscience at its best. The beast is dead; long live the beast! The adrenaline orgy should be subsiding soon, and now we must perform the ultimate moral duty of processing the sacred beast which has sacrificed its being for our life. Each kill is not so much an accomplishment as it is a gift from the Creator for a job well done. The heightened, optimum level of awareness that facilitated our effective predatorship to make a clean kill will now guide us to show reverence for the gift of delicious protein we must now turn into family-sized portions. This intense party of self-sufficiency continues and gets better yet. Since we hunters are face-to-face with the beast of our menu throughout the entire procurement process, there is no room for denial or excuse making. As it oughtta be.

With the quick, clean kill, comes a quick, efficient recovery of the animal, thereby minimizing the time from death to butchering. This sequence of time is the most critical in determining the quality tablefare that our precious meat will ultimately provide. It is this reasoning predatorship conscientiousness that drives man the hunter to think out each hunt and kill, therefor being far more effective and responsible in our killing efforts. Other than man, the reasoning predator, there are no beasts that have perfected mass slaughter assemblylines to feed all the critters. That is why there is still so much starvation in the wild. Meanwhile, we salute the farmers of America who feed the world with their fantastic system of food production. This same intellectual capability is implemented in its ultimate form when hunters dedicate such extensive time and effort to practice with their guns and bows to achieve such gratifying levels of proficiency in order to kill the beast with a single shot. Unlike the cheetah and lion and all other animal predators, we feel sadness and regret, if not downright anger, when we blow the shot, tormenting ourselves for extended periods of time afterwards for such failing. This sense of failure drives us to try harder to consummate the quick, clean kill that is the battlecry of hunters everywhere. Proficiency is everything. With hogs, butchering and cooking is more demanding than the procedure for venison from deer. With pigs, like bears and rabbits, the danger of trichinosis demands certain specialized procedures. The carcass must be thoroughly cleaned and immediately cooled and kept cool, certainly under 40 degrees Fahrenheit. Then the meat must be cooked thoroughly beyond medium to well done. This is why I cook pork and bear slower and longer, getting the internal temperature of the cooked flesh consistent to the core. Facing a pissed-off wild boar is good-scary. Eating undercooked pork is bad-scary.

The almighty backstrap on big game is sacred flesh. Commonly called pork tenderloin, this long, delectable strip of pure flesh is easily sliced from the underside of the backbone all the way from the rear of the shoulder to the top of the hips. A short, stout, 3- to 4-inch pocketknife blade is all you need to perform this sacred surgery, pulling the solid slab of meat from the backbone and the top of the ribs, slowly peeling it away from its moorings by separating it as much with fingertips as with the knife. It's the mark of a true animal lover when the mystical backstrap is removed and white rib bone and spine are visible. Did I mention lately how much I love animals? They're delicious.

Once removed, and after a few moments of indulgent, celebratory fondling of this wonderful slabbage just to feel its undulating protein in my loving fingertips, I then lay it down on my cutting board for the removal of any silver membrane and cartilage. Unlike deer venison, pork fat is truly desirable, providing a wonderful, sweet, tangy flavor boost to the meal. Therefor I do leave some fat on each piece, sometimes more than a little. Even on big, old gnarly boarhog swampbeasts, this porkfat is a real bonus for the tastebuds. And because it is wildgame, the fat does not retain and contain the animal's lifelong accumulation of chemicals and other undesirables as is found in domestic flesh. Like wild salmon versus fishfarm salmon, the best protein and nourishment comes from this natural, organic fatty tissue. That's why Inuit peoples have always lived longer and healthier from the quality fat reserves they build up in preparation for long winters.

Quite honestly, there is no bad way to prepare wildmeat. Just add fire and go wild! But my favorite porkfeast is real simple.

Ted's Favorite Porkfeast

I take the succulent strap, either whole or cut into individual 5-inch lengths per person, and set them on a double
layer of aluminum foil. I then coat each piece with a shimmer of olive oil, a little garlic salt, and a lot of garlic pepper. I add 2 or 3 whole, peeled white and red onions, a
half dozen whole red potatoes with the skins on, carrots,
clean celery stalks, a splash of white wine, and some
mashed cloves of garlic. I roll the foil up and around the
whole wad, but not too tightly in order to allow some air
circulation, and I set this delectable timebomb over some
red, glowing charcoal or wood embers. It is important to
keep this package away from direct flame so the slow
cooking process can do its magic. Occasionally checking
the fire will direct you to rake fresh, hot coals under the
package, keeping the heat medium and consistent. The
whole cooking time will be about 3 to 4 hours till the meat
is somewhat crusted and all the vegetables are cooked and
blended. The meat will literally fall apart and create a phenomenal pool of ultimate chow with the entire contents.
It's truly amazing.

Or, try it this way . . .

Maple-Bourbon Wild Boar

1 1-pound wild boar tenderloin, all visible fat removed
⅓ cup maple syrup
⅓ cup bourbon or unsweetened apple juice
2 tablespoons whole grain or Dijon mustard
2 tablespoons ketchup
Vegetable oil spray

Cut the wild boar into 12 medallions and flatten each
with the palm of your hand to about ¾-inch thickness. Set
aside. In a small bowl, stir together remaining ingredients
except vegetable oil spray. Set aside. Spray a large skillet
with the vegetable oil and place over medium-high heat.
Add 6 wild boar slices to hot skillet and cook for 3 minutes on each side or until slightly pink. Remove from skillet and keep warm. Repeat with remaining wild boar
slices. Add syrup mixture to skillet. Return to medium-
high heat, cook, and stir until bubbly, about 7 minutes.
Serve sauce with tenderloin. Serves 4.

11

THE BIG KAHUNA
by Shemane

We all do some pretty outrageous things for love, but lying on the ground twenty feet away from several massive North American bison has to take the cake. It was just after Ted and I eloped to Reno during the Shooting, Hunting, Outdoor Trade (SHOT) show, when he convinced me to spend the days following our wedding (also known as a honeymoon—or hunt-ingmoon) at the Y.O. Ranch in Texas. Looking back (and as a warning for all future hunting widows), I should have said no and opted for Hawaii. Like many women who eventually find themselves being pulled kicking and screaming into a hunting camp, my lovesick, rose-colored glasses painted a pretty picture. *Anywhere my husband goes, I'll go,* I remember thinking, and I donned baggy camouflage from head to toe and followed my groom into the vast Texas wilderness.

My having operated a small video production company just before we got married proved to be quite a perk for Ted. *"Just lie on the ground here and videotape me hunting out of this tree over there,"* he instructed me. The darn rose-colored glasses I was wearing really clouded my vision because in the distance I saw a herd of huge buffalo making their way down a heavily-traveled path right next to Ted's treestand, and less than a stone's throw from me. Surely, my new husband wouldn't put me in harm's way. *Surely.*

Nestled into his treestand with bow and quiver in hand, Ted scanned the great Texas hill country for a probable player in his game of hide and seek. When we first married, hunting was new to me, but I vowed to keep an open mind about the origins of my dinner. Ted assured me that a hunting trip would be a wonderful, romantic getaway unlike any other I had ever experienced. It turned out. . . he was right.

This was my first truly spiritual awakening experience. Sure, I had been out in the woods plenty of times, especially in my youth, but I do not recall having ever been so captivated by the sights, smells, and sounds of nature. We had become part of the trees and swayed with the wind, part of the ground as we remained calm and observant, and part of the air with minimal traces of human scent. We became *one* with Mother Nature. Every subtle movement or change in the temperature and setting appeared to be magnified tenfold.

The cold, hard ground was unforgiving, and I readjusted my position ever so slightly and ever so cautiously to compensate for my hips digging into the dirt. My body was stiff, but, no matter what, I vowed not to complain. My video camera was ready for action. Batteries charged. Plenty of tape.

At that point it occurred to me that the target of my new husband's affection was not me, but the two-ton behemoths making their way towards us. It also occurred to me that I was on the ground where they would quite possibly be headed. *What if they came directly toward me? Would Ted save me? Would I be stomped to death?* Now was not the time to ask. As the massive wads of fur and horn drew closer and closer, I was certain that everyone, Ted, the bison, and any wildlife in the near vicinity could hear my heart thumping its way out of my chest.

Camera on. Tape check. Battery check. Zoom in on steam fuming from bison's nostrils.

Ted's eyes grew larger as the small herd of great beasts was now 20 yards away. They stopped momentarily and lifted their colossal heads to the sky as if they caught a smell traveling past their snouts. We were so close that I could see their eyes move from side to side. *Something was up. Time stopped.* I held my breath.

To make things worse, my video camera made a startling and noisy humming sound when I began to record their images. But nothing could have prepared me for the moment the lead bison—*the Big Kahuna*—looked me right in the eye. My stomach knotted up and my arms and legs were numb and paralyzed with fear. *I had been found.* The Big Kahuna grunted and kept walking *right toward me.*

He was pissed!

I didn't know if Ted was aware of what had just taken place. His eyes were fixed on the target. He began to draw his bow. My camera zoomed in on his steadfast expression and then *ever so slowly* moved to the beast, which was staring intently at me. I heard Ted's bowstring whisper softly, just enough for the Big Kahuna to stop and present the perfect broadside shot. Then, swiftly, Ted's arrow bolted from the bow and shot right through the bison's heart. Startled by the sudden convulsion of their leader, the herd charged . . . *past* me.

Every time I think about my first hunting adventure, I realize how my life has become more vibrant and organic because of my outdoor experiences. Now I have a fresh appreciation for all that God has created. *"Every moving thing that liveth shall be meat for you"* (Gen. 9:3) is a Bible verse that has further confirmed my belief that a hunting lifestyle is honorable and good. Only after I witnessed the true cycle of life and death in the great outdoors could I understand the connection we all have with nature. I appreciate that relationship even more each time our family is seated at the dinner table.

Buffalo Loin with Morels

This recipe also works well with moose, elk, and caribou!

1 1-pound buffalo loin, cut into two 8-ounce steaks
Salt and pepper
3 tablespoons cooking oil
1 tablespoon chopped shallots
½ pound clean, sliced morels
½ cup chicken stock
½ cup white wine
1 cup heavy cream

Season buffalo with salt and pepper. In a large skillet (cast iron recommended), heat cooking oil, add steaks, cook to desired doneness (medium rare is preferred), and remove. Sweat chopped shallots in the skillet for 1 minute. Add sliced morels and cook for 1 minute more. Add chicken stock and white wine and bring to a boil. Cook over high heat for approximately 6 minutes or until liquid is reduced by half. Add heavy cream and heat for approximately 5 minutes or until it reaches a sauce consistency. Season morels with salt and pepper. Serve buffalo steaks over morels. Serves 4 to 6.

12

KILLIN' AND GRILLIN' LARGE GAME IN AMERICA

The Spirits of the Hunt playfully, yet forcefully, shoved my face again into the pungent, wet Everglades muck, and I did not resist. In fact, I sucked it up for all it was worth, enjoying the entire nostril-flaring dynamo. Somewhere overhead a pair of noisy sandhill cranes cackled and whooped above my prostrate form, intolerant of my intrusion into their heretofore private wintering grounds. They had never had to deal with a six-foot-two crawling intruder before. They had never met anyone as bonkers for adventure as I, that's for sure. But ahead of me in the grassy clearing were the massive hulks of four monstrous water buffalo, the glaring morning Florida sun spanking them on the backsides, causing them to glow against the overnight dew. I carefully snuck a peekaboo from the wet ground and squirmed and quivered like a pointing dog with a facefull of hot quailstink. I was rockin'.

A white egret lighted upon the wide back of the nearest beast, just like the oxpeckers do on the backs of Cape buffalo in Africa. With everything unfolding around me, this sunrise had all the appearances of Africa. The jungle-like scrub of myrtle I had emerged from, the splattering of dense thickets against the savannah clearings, even the groves of vine-choked palmetto, oak, and palm trees gave an eerie Dark Continent graphic to the entire setting. But ultimately, it was the black hoary giants before me that clinched the outrageous exotica of it all. The massive, sweeping, threatening horns atop the ominous, hulking, mus-cled, tanklike flesh-and-blood herbivorous trucks were the defin-ing touch. At once, they proved to be every bit like the awesomely powerful and dangerous African Cape buffalo, when they abruptly lifted their giant heads straight up, heaved boulder-like shoulders back, and turned on a dime to defiantly face the pair of big worms that got just a little bit too close. And I mean too close for com-fort. I was anything but comfortable as I peeked below my hat-brim at the nearest beast, a scant ten yards above me. His huge bloodshot eyes bugged wildly and his flaring nostrils spit savage snot, trying to scent confirm what we were, as my cameraman Jim Lawson and I shook in our boots. Nailed! Dammit! Pissed-off buffalo are extremely impressive.

This was the tenth, long, wet bellycrawl stalk we had nearly succeeded at in two intense days of Asiatic buffalo hunting with Joe O'Bannon on his vast J&R Outfitters hunting grounds. Located a short swampdrive northwest of West Palm Beach, you would surely believe you were in a far-off exotic land once you left the overdeveloped concrete hell of most of tourist-infested Florida. It was wonderful. Flocks of many different, beautiful

Everglade birdlife soared here and there. Wild, impenetrable jungle-like vegetation punctuated the landscape. A distinct and purely wild aroma filled the air and life throbbed undeniably all around. We were compelled to move slowly if at all, driven to take in the whole wad.

As the beasto foursome spun and thundered off in a flash, we sat up to review the exciting morning encounter. They turned and faced us at about two hundred yards, standing defiantly and majestically in the rising sunglow. Each bull would weigh in excess of a ton apiece, and all four bulls wore sweeping, heavy horns that would surely qualify way up in the record books. We glassed them for quite awhile till they finally meandered off, then we refreshed ourselves with water and cheese to replenish the lost energy sucked from us in the rising Florida heat and the long, challenging sneak.

Having hunted Cape buffalo in Africa for more than twenty-two years, and loving every stupefying minute of it, I was amazed to discover the same adventure is available in America. Joe had developed and managed this unique population of pure Asian buffalo for years in order to bring the thrilling dynamic of dangerous game hunting to America. As a longtime licensed professional hunter in four African countries, he knew this specialized hunting opportunity would impress any hunter seeking the ultimate thrill in big game hunting. Not only that, but with the ugly development madhouse running amok throughout Florida, the future of wildground and wildlife is in the hands of true conservationist visionaries like Joe O'Bannon. Without hands-on appreciation for wild habitat and its wild inhabitants, I give you concrete mall, manicured golf course death. Buffalo hunting beats Disney all to hell.

After endless hours of intense glassing and many real close stalks, goodluck was ours in the eleventh hour when we saw three great bulls slowly feeding their way toward a vegetation-choked canal. Positioning ourselves within a shaded sand dune and behind a tangle of driftwood and stumps, the enormous lead trophy beast appeared at about 36 yards and hesitated before wading into the water. Unfortunately, my nerves were a disaster by then and my shot went low and left, slicing the herd bull below the vitals. In the heart hammering tradition of tracking wounded dangerous game, we eventually finished him off with a pair of .470 Nitro Express rounds and a hail of 10mm armor-piercing 180-grainers. He was a monster and a beauty. Joe was the consummate guide and backup, and Jim captured the entire ordeal on digital tape.

We conducted some arrow penetration tests on the huge bull, and were impressed with the effectiveness of my 440-grain carbon arrows. Flying around 220 fps from my 65# compound bow, my razorsharp Nugent Blade broadheads penetrated the full depth of the 30-inch wide chest cavity; slicing all vitals for a certain, quick kill. And that certain quick kill is just what the good buffalo doctor ordered for when I return to do it again. Soon! This may very well be the most exciting hunting to be had in North America today, and certainly makes for some delicious big game eatin'.

Big Game Meat Cakes

This is a good way to prepare the tougher cuts of buffalo, deer, elk, antelope, moose, and bear which the freezing plant or processor usually grinds for hunters.

1 teaspoon salt
½ teaspoon pepper
¼ cup catsup
¼ cup chopped onion
1 pound ground lean meat

In a large bowl, add salt, pepper, catsup, and onion to ground lean meat. Mix well, shape into small flat cakes, and cook in a hot greased skillet, usually about 4 minutes per side. One pound of lean meat will serve 2.

Bar-B-Que Black Bear

Sauce
¼ cup vinegar
½ cup water
2 tablespoons sugar
1 teaspoon dry mustard
½ teaspoon pepper
1½ teaspoons salt
¼ teaspoon garlic powder
1 teaspoon lemon juice
1 onion, minced
¼ cup salad oil
1 teaspoon chili powder
5 dashes Tabasco sauce
½ cup ketchup
2 tablespoons Worcestershire sauce

1- to 2-pound bear roast

Place all sauce ingredients in a blender and blend until smooth. Pour into a medium saucepan and simmer uncovered for 20 minutes. Add the ketchup and Worcestershire sauce, bring to a boil, and remove from heat. Preheat oven to 325 degrees. Place bear roast in a roasting pan and cook until well glazed, then baste with the sauce. Baste frequently and cook 3 to 4 hours (depending on size of roast) until tender.

Without hands-on
appreciation for wild
habitat and its wild
inhabitants, I give
you concrete mall,
manicured golf
course death.

13

I LIKE MINE RARE, BUT NOT THAT RARE

Drifting dust was gently parachuting back to the Good Mother Earth from the recoil of my 7mm Magnum rifleshot, and the beautiful echothump of 175 grains of copper-jacketed lead punching hard flesh and bone at 3,000 feet per second pumped back to me like an Ali jab to the gut. Already my two Watusi trackers were sprinting across the Sudanese veldt toward my downed, but still kicking, roan, a huge, beautiful horse-sized African antelope renowned for its escape and defensive capabilities and aggressive, tenacious attitude. I prayed for their safety and hoped it would die before they covered the 200 yards. I humped up from prone and mad dashed head on into their vaportrail, excited to touch the first ceremonious beast of my very first baptismal African Dream Safari. At this point, I was the totally prime rock 'n' roll athletic dynamo of thirty years of age, and I covered ground with the best of them, so I was even more surprised when

I quickly came upon my boys and witnessed an amazing ritual of the African Tooth, Fang, & Claw aboriginal existence. Though the one thousand-pound animal was technically finished, his still kicking hooves thrashed violently, tho intermittently, at the slicing natives as they slid their crude, long, homemade shivs deep into the belly of the huge bull. As a lifelong hunter myself, I insist on performing all the necessary, personal rituals of the sacred hunt, and therefor wished to gut the animal myself. But as they plunged their fists and arms deep into the fat belly, I didn't bother to stop them, because at once they extracted a handful of still pulsating red-purple liver the size of a seatcushion and held it up over their heads, blood oozing down upon them as they stood shoulder to shoulder. I watched, fascinated, my eyes bugging, predator mind taking it all in. With white teeth gleaming in the hot primordial sunglow, each man took turns slicing long, thin pieces of this vital filtering organ, then letting them slide down their throat whole, the entire time making happy, giddy, laughing, gulping noises. They looked to me as if to offer a taste, but tho brave I am, I held up my hand to say, "No thank you. You go right ahead. Your fresh liver breakfast is on me! I'll wait for fire and onions, thank you." And they call me the MotorCity MadMan! I had much to learn.

As a proud American hunter, fisherman, and trapper, I was raised to ultimately respect life by intelligently and conscientiously utilizing the precious life-giving renewable resources, particularly the amazing renewable wildlife resources, that God created to sustain us. Though my father, Warren Henry Nugent, taught me well to properly care for and use the game I bagged, my understanding of conservation was upgraded by these native warriors. I learned as I watched them put to use every last scrap of flesh, bone, sinew, hoof, skeleton, internal organ, body fluids, eyeballs, and everything else from every kill I made on this hunt. They actually rendered the stomach contents and rechewed them, even cleaning the stomach itself and cooking it up as a delicacy. You want "wise use," hunt with an aborigine. And if you want to cry, witness the vulgar waste of the average American family as they fail to use but the primecuts of flesh from sacrificial dead beasts, then have the audacity to toss out most of that precious commodity. I often feel like the Indian on horseback overlooking the littered landscape, deeply hurt at the sacrilege of our careless abuse of our earthly home.

I love fresh, and I insist on pure organic when I can get it, but this whiteboy was not quite ready for this abrupt spiritual swandive back to the lip of my ancestral cave just yet. I learned fast that tribes still living this timeless reality of true life and death survival in the sub-Saharan bush desperately need maximum protein, and would never dare miss an opportunity. These powerful lessons in real world reality were driven inescapably home to me for the next three weeks on this astonishing adventure in the wilds of the Sudan. In fact, I was faced with do or die, life and death maneuvers of my own on this safari, as the last whiteguy to get out of this part of Africa alive. I literally ran for my life from marauding gangs of murderous rebels, recently armed with unlimited AK47s and ammo by Idi Amin. I was led to safety by the native hunters I had befriended. We ran from Kapueta to Juba where I miraculously commandeered a Red Cross Piper that flew me to Cairo. I eventually made my way via London and New York to hit the stage at the Ontario Speedway in California, fifteen minutes late for my performance at Cal Jam II, where I insanely rocked three hundred thousand American rock 'n' roll maniacs, with African dirt and blood still on my boots and under my fingernails. "Cat Scratch Fever" never sounded so intense or natural. Fear, blood, guts, and the thrill of making it home alive makes for the ultimate R&B rock 'n' roll. Believe me.

With the unbelievable intensity of this African adventure came a gargantuan increase in my already intense craving for quality life, and how to best live it. The fascinating lifestyle of these fiercely independent, earthly people didn't exactly shock me from a citi-fied, insulated American lifestyle. I had hunted and fished my entire life, and was not only well aware of the precious cycle of life and death, I downright celebrated it hands on, killing all my family's meat with a bow and arrow and the powerful predator touch that bowhunting demanded. The natives in this harsh envi-ronment felt this spiritual kinship with the American longhaired guitarboy with the amazing modern compound bow and alu-minum arrows, and we spent some wonderful campfire time together. We were, afterall, BloodBrothers of the sharp stick.

I went on to bowkill a number of African game on this safari, including the diminutive dik-dik antelope, warthog, and two mon-strous Cape buffalo. I also took waterbuck, lesser kudu, roan, Lord Derby eland, white-eared kob, many Grant's gazelle, tiang, lion, a third Cape buffalo, and more dik-dik with my Browning 7 Mag loaded with Remington 175-grain Core-Lokt ammo. It was a mezmerizing, all-consuming hunt that I will never forget. Each night we would dine on the succulent, delicious flesh of each day's kills, augmented by the timeless medicine of the Great Hunt.

You want wholefoods! I got your ultimate wholefoods right here.

The mighty sniper .243 brings pure venison to ground once again.

The Spirit of the Bear provides grand, delicious protein for the belly and the soul.

Sunrize Acres is home to the biggest, baddest, most delicious Russian Pork in America.

The Queen of the Forest can bring home the bacon any ol' time.

Ah, the Mystical Flight of her arrow truly turns me on.

Small game, big food.

A perfect Nugent hole in one!

Squirrel boys collect another limbrat for the pot.

Gonzo and Ted, cocks in hand.

Mallards: real fast food.

One thousand pounds of pure sustenance: North American Wapiti.

Muskox. Alaska. 70 below.

Bob Foulkrod, Ted, and Quebec trout.

Nomadic steaks. Quebec Labrador caribou.

Toby Nugent and his recordbook beast.

Ted, Shemane, and Rocco.

Sonic Bombast.

Rocco's 2002 beast.

Texas BBQ.

Tribe Nuge.

Shemane and Y.O. Fallow Buck.

Nugents Afield!

Shemane and Gram.

Sweet 'n' Sour Antelope

Try this recipe with elk, moose, and other big game, too!

1-pound antelope round steak, cut into strips
¼ cup soy sauce
1¾ cups water
1 teaspoon salt (optional)
1 whole garlic clove
¼ cup cider vinegar
⅓ cup pineapple juice
⅓ cup white granulated sugar
¼ cup cornstarch
¼ teaspoon ground ginger
¾ cup pineapple chunks
1 whole green pepper, diced

Place antelope strips in a two-quart saucepan with soy sauce, water, salt, and garlic and bring to a boil over high heat. Cover pan, reduce heat, and simmer 12 to 15 minutes or until meat is just cooked. Remove antelope strips and set aside. Strain broth through cheesecloth or coffee filter, reserving broth! In a large saucepan, add the vinegar, pineapple juice, sugar, cornstarch, and ginger and stir until smooth. Slowly stir in reserved broth, mixing well. Cook over high heat, stirring often for approximately 6 to 8 minutes, or until sauce thickens and becomes transparent. Add antelope strips, pineapple chunks, and green pepper to sauce. Remove from heat and let stand a few minutes before serving. Serve over white rice. Enjoy!

Wild Sheep Shanks

6 sheep shanks, approximately 1 pound each
Pepper and kosher salt
2 to 3 cups flour
½ cup olive oil
1 onion, peeled and diced
1 carrot, peeled and sliced
2 celery stalks, trimmed and diced
½ fennel bulb, sliced
2 cups white wine
6 tablespoons Dijon mustard
1 to 2 bay leaves
Wad of peppercorns
1 head garlic, peeled, cut in half
6 cups lamb stock or chicken broth

Season shanks with salt and pepper and dust with flour.
Reserve flour. Heat olive oil in a large pan and sear
shanks until golden brown. Add the onion, carrot, celery,
and fennel to the pan in which the shanks were seared
and sauté until soft. Add reserved flour to vegetables and
cook until golden. Add white wine and reduce by half.

Add mustard, bay leaves, peppercorns, garlic, and stock. Bring to a boil. Pour vegetable mixture over shanks and place in a 400 degree oven and cook until very tender, turning shanks every hour. Remove shanks from liquid and strain. Place pan on top of stove and reduce liquid until thickened, it should be thick enough to coat a spoon. Adjust seasonings and skim off fat. Uncover last 5 to 10 minutes. Place shanks on plate and serve surrounded with roasted potatoes. Drizzle a little sauce over shanks and potatoes. (To reheat shanks that have been refrigerated, put shanks in covered pan with a little water for about half an hour.) Serves 6.

African Sheep Steaks

4 sheep round steaks
½ to ⅓ cup flour
1 teaspoon seasoned salt
½ teaspoon pepper
¼ cup butter
1 medium onion, sliced in rings
2 cups tomato sauce
2 tomatoes, chopped
2 teaspoons sugar
1 teaspoon dried basil
1 teaspoon parsley flakes
½ teaspoon celery seed
½ cup water
1 tablespoon Worcestershire sauce
2 teaspoons instant beef bouillon

Remove fat and bone from steaks and cut in half. Combine flour, salt, and pepper, dust steaks, then pound flour mixture into both sides of steaks until all of the flour mixture is used. Melt the butter in a skillet, add the steaks, and cook until well browned on both sides. Push meat to one side, add onion rings, and lightly brown. Move sheep steaks to a single layer and place onion rings on top. Combine tomato sauce, tomatoes, sugar, basil, parsley, celery seed, water, Worcestershire sauce, and beef bouillon in a bowl and mix well. Pour sauce over meat, lower heat, cover, and simmer for 1 hour or until meat is tender. Serves 4 to 6.

Coca-Cola Stew
by Shemane

So many people ask me what I do to tenderize wild game—this is one of the few marinades I use. The acid in the Coca-Cola softens the meat and sweetens it, too. This is absolutely my favorite dish! I love it because you can throw everything into a crock-pot in the morning and return to discover the most tender and delectable-tasting, candied meat you've ever tasted! We serve this during each Queen of the Forest camp and everyone loves it. Try it and let us know if it becomes your favorite, too!

1 venison backstrap
2 cans Coca-Cola
4 to 6 potatoes, diced
4 to 6 carrots, peeled and quartered
1 yellow onion, sliced
1 jar of sweet chutney
Water, enough to cover meat
Salt and pepper to taste

You don't need to slice up the meat, but sear it first before putting it into the crock-pot. Place all ingredients in a crock-pot, turn on low, cover, and go shopping for 4 hours! Return to a delicious meal that tastes as though you slaved over a hot stove all day.

CHAPTER

14

ON THE SWEETER SIDE . . .
by Shemane

From certain perspectives, Ted and I might seem completely mismatched. After all, when we first met I was the traffic reporter at a rock 'n' roll radio station, but I didn't actually listen to the music. I preferred Top 40 hits. Not only would I have failed "Rock & Roll Jeopardy," I couldn't even tell the difference between a Gibson Les Paul and a Byrdland, a Glock and a revolver, or a kudu and a gemsbok. Now, however, twelve years after Ted and I became legally bound and passionately inseparable, I can easily distinguish them from one another about as fast as Ted can draw a gun and shoot. Ted still finds it deplorable that I made it through twenty-six hunting seasons without knowing anyone who actually went hunting. *Imagine!* Neither my father nor my brother hunted, and before I met Ted, I wouldn't have been able to sing "Cat Scratch Fever" if my life depended on it.

But looking back I realize my childhood had perfectly prepared me for the role as Mrs. Nugent, the *MotorCity MadMan's
wife*. As an eager little sister who tried everything her older brother
did, I raced motorcycles and four-wheelers, spent lots of time
outdoors, and although I never knew a thing about hunting and
very little of fishing, I always wanted to be in the woods. The
neighborhood kids and I spent as many hours as possible exploring the vacant, wooded lots that peppered the landscape of our
suburban neighborhood. I loved getting my hands dirty. I loved
animals. I tried every sport there was, and by the time I was twelve,
I had over one hundred medals, ribbons, and trophies as a state
champion swimmer.

This would soon prove to be important in *Ted's World* because
there is no room for whiners. No room for underachievers. We
Nugents do it all, and that is one of the most gratifying aspects of
my life. There is rarely a lackluster moment. The entire Nugent
family is involved in some aspect of our numerous ventures, from
our weekly *Spirit of the Wild* television show that Ted and I write,
edit, produce, and videotape ourselves, to the tednugent.com Web
site, to *Ted Nugent Adventure Outdoors*, our bi-monthly maga-
zine. We've even put young Rocco to work with his very own
"Kid's Korner" segment on our television show. Before the sun
rises, I've already put in an hour or two of editing the show, and
when Ted's on tour, it's not unusual for us to be in two or even
three different states in one day. We often meet with a variety of
people, too. In a twenty-four hour period we could be strategizing with political acquaintances, doing the Howard Stern show,
or meeting with our son's teacher. The downside is, well, we have
little downtime, and that's exactly why we take great pride in

cooking wholesome food and reserving dinnertime for family discussions.

The velocity at which we travel, live, and work would leave most Indy 500 racers in the dust. We *have* to be healthy in order to maintain the frenzied pace in which we rip through our calendar pages. What keeps us going? It's simple. Good food. Food that's not laden with chemicals and steroids. We eat wild game that is lean and pure. We avoid fast food that can clog arteries, cause weight gain, and sap energy. Good food fuels us and keeps us healthy so that we can work hard and continually strive toward greater accomplishments.

It is all about getting back to the basics of eating—naturally. The closer we can get to eating fruit from the tree, meat off the hoof, or vegetables from the ground, the better. Our ancestors were hunters and gatherers. That's how our bodies were designed to function. Unfortunately, we have gone so far away from this fundamental means of procurement. Today, much of what we ingest has been loaded with chemicals and toxins, which eventually wreak havoc on our digestive systems and the basic healthy blueprint for the human body. Medical books and journals substantiate the theory that what ails us today, from migraines to cancer, may be caused by us, possibly at our own inadvertent requests. We demand that millions of chickens and cows be slaughtered each day and shipped to our grocers. We want eggs, and lots of them! But food poisoning is the price we pay to have slabs of meat butchered and wrapped for us by the ton—hundreds of thousands of people become sick each day. According to the Centers for Disease Control (CDC), seventy-six million people are stricken by food borne illnesses each year. While most food poisoning results in abdominal cramping, diarrhea, and fever, some, like infants and seniors get hit worse. *Five thousand* people die each year from food poisoning.

Those of us who have had chronic ailments understand best that you cannot accomplish a thing when you don't feel good. For more than a decade, I have suffered from serious, debilitating migraines where I find myself hospitalized at least once a year. To date there is no cure for migraines other than taking preventative medication, avoiding certain "triggers" like too much caffeine, peanuts, or monosodium glutamate (MSG), and avoiding stress (do you know who my husband is?). Needless to say, I have exhaustively searched for a treatment or some way to alleviate the excruciating pain I, and millions of others, experience all too often. During my investigation, I have learned much about living a more healthy life that consists mostly of good nutrition and exercise. Eating whole, natural foods, not processed and packaged, will help you live a longer, more productive life. My migraines are under control when I eat fresh rather than frozen or canned foods. It's in the details—I read labels and find out what's in that sloppy joe mix. If you cannot pronounce it, chances are it is not *real food*. Instead, it could be a radically altered man-made substance designed to take on the taste and appearance of what we know to be food. Preservatives designed to prolong so-called "food" can cause toxic buildup within intestinal walls and, as we now know, lead to cancer. Packaged foods like macaroni and cheese and other boxed meals that require adding water and meat are intended to stay on shelves for months, sometimes even years. Is that the best way to fuel your body? I am proud of the fact that our family lives off the land. Never buying meat from the store, we eat what we harvest ourselves. We know everything about our food.

There's never been a better time than now to eat wild game. The United States Department of Agriculture has declared that all commercial poultry has some percentage of salmonella poisoning. However, there are few, if any, documented cases of any type of bacterial poisoning in venison or other wild game. We enjoy life to the fullest here at the Nugent ranch, and we don't crack the whip twenty-four hours a day. There are some vacillations. I have been known to make lusciously soft and fluffy chocolate chip cookies or brownies for Rocco and his friends. (When they're not looking I even add a little whole-wheat flour.) Ted and I indulge on special occasions and enjoy delicious desserts at fabulous restaurants when we travel, or a scoop or two of Häagen Dazs Chocolate Chocolate Chip ice cream. Knowledge and moderation is our formula for eating well and enjoying it—and that includes dessert! 犬

Mom's Blintzes
by Shemane

Rarely a Sunday morning goes by when Ted doesn't beg me to make the same blintzes his mother, Marion, used to make for him when he was a little boy. Just before she passed away, she gave me this delicious recipe handwritten on a 3 x 5 index card. It will forever remind Ted of some youthful indulgences, and I will cherish it always. It's one of those dishes that's loaded with love and calories!

4 eggs
8 tablespoons flour
1 cup milk
1 teaspoon salt
Melted butter or cooking spray
8 tablespoons cottage cheese
4 tablespoons sour cream
Powdered sugar

Beat first four ingredients in a standing mixer. Coat a 6- to 8-inch nonstick pan with a little melted butter or cooking spray and heat over medium-high heat. Pour about ¼ cup of batter into the hot pan and swirl it around so that it coats the entire bottom.

When the batter begins to stiffen and bubble, add approximately 2 tablespoons of cottage cheese and smooth out into a thin strip along the center. (This is to heat up the cottage cheese a bit.) Next, fold in the edges with a spatula and (if you properly greased the pan) you'll be able to slide the blintz right onto a plate. Immediately smear a tablespoon or two of sour cream on top of the blintz and sprinkle with enough powdered sugar to make your sweet tooth disappear for a week! Makes 4 blintzes.

Banana and Chocolate Crepes
by Shemane

I discovered this incredibly sensuous dessert after experimenting with the *Mom's Blintzes* recipe. It is based on a dessert from one of our favorite restaurants, Caviarteria in Las Vegas. Just add a bit more milk to thin the blintz batter, substitute thin slices of bananas and Hershey's syrup for the cottage cheese, and finish with just a little more chocolate syrup and loads of whipped cream. Oh, and ladies, you'll need high heels and a nightie to serve this.

CHAPTER

15

HASENPFEFFER BY GLOCK

With more snow and colder temperatures in this month of December than during any other year on record in Michigan, the critters had some intense life and death survival challenges in their faces. There is much contention even in the scientific community over whether man should help feed weather-threatened wildlife, but in my fifty-three years, I have drawn my own conclusions based on my own real-world, hands-on relationship with all the animals in my life. Like a birdfeeder in the yard, a deerfeeder at swampsedge can bring amazing joy to the wildlife lover. It is their increased visibility that drives us to feed animals and watch them, making us more a part of their magical world. It's wild and I love it. Each day I load up the array of backyard birdfeeders with sunflower seeds, suet blocks, and birdmix, and then throw out a bag of shellcorn and some alfalfa hay for the squirrels and rabbits. They actually join me on the deck, and it is always fascinating to be so close to wild critters. Even deer wander into the yard each evening before dark to join the festivities, and it is a wildlife feeding frenzy spectacle. I spread the feed all around to minimize the natural fighting propensity of the competitive menagerie. We don't hunt or shoot near the house, so it represents a safehaven sanctuary for all the animals. It is all very gratifying. Of course some birds of prey don't abide by our reasoning predator rules, and we get to witness Ma Nature's thrilling Tooth, Fang, and Claw reality check every once in awhile in a flurry of feathers and blood. The children find it especially informative and exciting. Hawks are fast and savage! And cool.

On one snowmobile snowfield run to put out wildlife protein blocks, I sledded (slowly and cautiously—snowmobiles do not have to be as intrusive or dangerous as some make them seem) past my old favorite hellhole of briars and brambles and multiflora rose puckerbrush noman's tangleland rabbit heaven. As the late afternoon winter sun snuck a peek from behind the dark January clouds, a sea of various animal tracks glistened on the pure white snow, appearing like shadowy etchings on a topographical artistic landscape. I just had to shut off the machine and stop to examine its beauty in detail. Fox squirrels and red squirrels had scampered here and there amongst the grove of oak trees, and deertracks were everywhere. The snow was swept away at the base of a cherry tree where a hawk or an owl had killed a rabbit. Splashes of red and tufts of gray hairs told the timeless drama of life and death in the wild. Tiny fieldmouse tracks lined out looping and circling, apparent directionless wanderings from one clump of vegetation to another; and a pair of fox had investigated this wildlife pantry recently as well. As I walked along, the activities of many days gone by were spelled out before me in graphic detail, with tracks from a dog, cat, turkeys, coyote, and mink clearly imprinted in the snow. I squatted and read the best book in the world. The story was compelling and the pictures were awesome!

As I took it all in, I noticed that some of the rabbit tracks were very fresh, and my mind responded to the flavor of the dynamic, natural setting. A pure, raw-nerved predator twitch stood me upright. Like the fox and coyote, I knew it was rabbit hunting season, and I was in the epicenter of Bunnyland USA! With my rabbit fur hat earflaps pulled down tight, I unzipped my old Ducks Unlimited full-length parka halfway, reached deep into my insulated coveralls for my Galco shoulder holster, and filled my hand with Glock 10mm cottontail medicine. Though this is not my favorite rabbit gun (I do most of my smallgame hunting with a .22 revolver), I more often than not find myself in good game-cover as I perform my daily ranch chores, and this gun I carry is the most practical option. Not only that, but anyone who is thoughtful and responsible enough to carry a gun for self-defense will take advantage of every opportunity to practice and build confidence with that particular arm. And no shooting practice exists that develops hand-eye tactical proficiency like hitting a fleeing, hopping, zigzagging, bouncing bunny rabbit. It's almost impossible, but an absolute riot trying.

My first long step into the thicket brought powdery snow over the top of my LaCrosse boots, and a swaying arm of multiflora rose snagged my sleeve. Immediately beneath the overhanging brush burst an exploding ball of fur, and instinctively my handgun swung smoothly up and behind the speeding target. Amazingly my first round of a doubletap busted the rabbit in midleap, the second shot blowing snowdust all around the

Rabbit Track Soup

The perfect recipe! 0 grams fat, 0 grams sodium, 0 grams cholesterol, 0 calories.

24 sets of prime Upper Peninsula rabbit tracks imbedded in at least 3 inches of fresh snow.

Using a large, flat shovel, carefully remove top two inches of snow containing rabbit tracks and place in a well-scrubbed bucket. Make sure the snow is white (not yellow) and free of small, dark, round objects or other debris. Place the snow in a 6-quart soup kettle and heat on medium high to the desired temperature. Serve in dark bowls for contrast with the snowy white soup. May be garnished with a pinch of north wind.

rolling bunny. The 135-grain bullet had clipped the top of the cottontail's shoulders and killed him instantly. With my boot still stuck in the snow, I just grinned wildly at the surprising shot. I manage to handgun few rabbits every year on the run, but it is always a thrill to do so. Most of my handgun kills are on stationary targets where I get ample time to sight carefully or even employ a solid rest. But there he was, and I picked up my first rabbit of the day.

It turned out to be my only rabbit of the day as I managed to cleanly miss the next three, all sitting shots at various ranges. But I sure had a hoot busting through the nastiest brush a guy would dare try, exploring mind-bogglingly beautiful countryside, and breathing in the bold, delicious winter air of my precious wild. I ended up putting out a lot of supplemental gamefeed that day, seeing a dazzling array of beautiful wildlife, and feeling the Great Spirit of the Wild in all her winter, water, wonderland glory. The best "other" white meat made for a special dinner that night, and the woodstove felt a little warmer to this old rabbit hunter.

Rabbit Belle Chasse

3 small rabbits, cut into approximately 6 pieces
1 to 2 lemons
Flour for dredging
Salt and pepper to taste
A spit more than a shimmer (1 to 2 tablespoons)
    of peanut oil
Wad of sour cream

Rub rabbits with lemon and refrigerate overnight. Wipe rabbits with a damp cloth and sprinkle with salt and pepper. Roll rabbits in flour and sear in a hot skillet with the peanut oil until browned on both sides. Place in a baking dish, cover with sour cream, and bake at 350 degrees for about 30 minutes. Serve on a bed of rice.

Sweet 'n' Sticky Rabbit

1 cup honey
Juice of 1 lemon
1 teaspoon prepared mustard
Paprika
2 rabbits, cut up
2 tablespoons melted butter or margarine
Parsley for garnish

Preheat broiler to 550 degrees. In a small sauce pan, combine honey, lemon juice, and mustard. Stir over medium heat until hot and well mixed. Remove from heat and set aside. Rub paprika all over rabbit pieces. Place rabbit on broiler pan and brush with melted butter. Place rabbit 5 to 7 inches from heat and brown on both sides for 5 to 7 minutes. Remove from broiler and place rabbit in a casserole dish. Pour the honey, lemon, and mustard sauce over the rabbit, cover, and bake 35 to 40 minutes at 325 degrees. Remove from oven and serve on platter garnished with parsley. Serve with potato salad and corn.

Like a birdfeeder in the yard, a deerfeeder at swampsedge can bring amazing joy to the wildlife lover. Their increased visibility drives us to feed animals and watch them, making us more a part of their magical world.

CHAPTER

16

LIMBRAT ÉTOUFFÉE

Kill tree-dwelling vermin, remove PJs, take to flame, chowdown. Drive safely. It's really that simple to get a good meal of squirrel. Limbrat whackin' is truly bigfun any ol' way ya choose it—bow and arrow, pistol, rifle, scattergun, slingshot, falconry, grenades, and my favorite, flamethrower. How can ya go wrong? Squirrels are, afterall, rodents, so have fun blasting away. That there exists a season or baglimit on the little shits is mind-boggling to say the least. Winterstorms and extended subzero conditions kill more squirrels than any hunting ever could. Annual starvation keeps em trimmed down pretty darn good, but there never seems to be a shortage of the little rascals in borderline farm or timber country. I love huntin' em and eatin' em. It's like freerange chicken with attitude. Hell, a country and western drunk biker that eats that many acorns would probably crisp up pretty yummy. Let the bushytail games begin!

My alltime favorite squirrel prep is to eat em fresh at Au Sable River's edge, following one of my spiritual orgies of the mighty Michigan outback. Washed clean in the flowing water, then roasted over an open fire on a crisp, cold, clear moonlit October eve, and you live a powerful slice of heaven on earth.

I also enjoy em marinated overnite in French salad dressing, then olive oiling em up real good and roasting em over hot coals with lemon pepper and garlic salt. Deeelicious!

But if you're hankerin' for a real treat, roll up your gumbo Zodiki sleeves like a coonass in heat and swandive into a big Delta estuary for some fingerlickin' good Cajun delight. Ladies and gentlemen, start your crock-pots!

Heat up that big ol' crock-pot on high with a stick of real butter to melt while you're browning your 2 to 3 squirrel carcasses in hot olive oil. Ya may as well fill the squirrel skillet with diced onions while ya singe the meat as it makes a wonderful bonus bath of flavor. Deposit the deboned and flaked singed meat and reduced onions into the bottom of the crock-pot as the butter becomes liquid, then cover this layer with diced celery, a thin layer of parsley flakes, diced onions, parsley flakes again, celery, onions, parsley, then a wad of cooked white rice. Add to this a few tablespoons of soy sauce and a few shakes of garlic pepper and garlic salt. Suck maximum flavored air.

Now add a cup of white wine and a cup of water, reduce the heat to simmer, and go hunting for a few hours. This brew should simmer and undulate like spawning luvslugs for about 3 to 6 hours at the lowest heat, but not stirred till just before serving time. I suppose you could use any good dead flesh, but there's something about the ecstasy of squirrel hunting with your son, the sneaky stalk to catch em off guard, the dead-on accurate marxmanship challenge of a handy little .22 rifle, the beauty of the woods, and certainly the profound spirit of killing your own food. Anyway ya cut it, this dish will leave you feeling mighty fine and ready to do it all over again. Do it all over again. Or try the limbrats casserole style. It's a Tribe Nuge favorite and finger-lickin' good—the Colonel's got nothing on this.

Squirrel Casserole

2 squirrels
2 10-ounce packages frozen broccoli with cheese
1 stick butter or margarine
1 cup chopped onion
1 cup chopped celery
1 10¾-ounce can cream of mushroom soup, undiluted
1 cup cooked rice
Dash of garlic powder
Salt and pepper to taste

In a saucepan, cover squirrels with water, and boil until meat is tender and falls from bones. Cook broccoli according to package directions. Melt butter over medium heat in a skillet, add onion and celery, and sauté until tender. Add the soup and stir well. Combine squirrel, broccoli mixture, and rice in a 13" x 9" inch baking dish. Season with garlic powder, salt, and pepper. Bake at 350 degrees for 1 hour.

Kill tree-dwelling
vermin, remove PJs,
take to flame, chow-
down. Drive safely.
It's really that simple
to get a good meal
of squirrel.

17

BUSHYTAIL BUSHWHACKIN'

love a good belly-krankin', Full Bluntal Nugity laugh. My twelve-arrow Sagittarius assault-bowquiver was now completely empty of feathered shafts, but all I could do was laugh out loud and shake my head in total hysterics. It's never funny being out of ammo, but this was truly humorous. One big, fat bushytailed fox squirrel dangled from the stratospheric oak-limb towering overhead, still just picking away at the clumps of juicy acorns around him without a care in the animal world. I swear I heard him chuckle along with me. And if I'm not mistaken, I could swear he separated the middle toe from the others on his front foot and flipped it my way. It sure looked like it! And combined with that nut-chompin', toothy Cheshire grin on his face, I am almost certain he was trying to tell me something deep and profound, as far as rodents go. I believe that his chatter can be loosely translated from squirrel speak to English as, "buy chicken whiteboy!" Damn limbrats!

I had started out with ultrahigh hopes at dawn, once again on my sacred annual Michigan September squirrel hunt, bow and lots of arrows in hand. Now I'm well aware that bowhunting for squirrels could, more often than not, send a guy scrambling for the chicken counter at the local grocery store, but I'm an adventurous kind of guy, always seeking that road less traveled and exploration sometimes less smart. And there are few things less smart than trying to hit a squirrel with an arrow. It is always a barrel of fun to stillhunt for smallgame with a shotgun, .22 rifle, or handgun, but the archery challenge cannot be beat. I never said I was smart, just adventurous.

Typically, I bring home a few squirrels per outing, often supplemented with the occasional rabbit or even the rare pheasant or quail that I may get a crack at. It is a fascinating challenge, stalking along ever so silently and slowly catching these amazingly wary, constantly hunted smaller animals off guard and getting an arrow away at them. When I actually hit em and bring em to bag, it is truly a grand cause célèbre. But more often than not I merely make another investment in the arrow manufacturing industry, to which I am without question the most generous provider. Thar's feathered aluminum and carbon in them thar hills partner! Lots! Of course, if I am bowhunting on farmground, I make maximum effort to retrieve my every arrow so as to eliminate the chance of a farmer's tractor or equipment encountering the shaft or arrowhead. And if I'm hunting wherever arrowflight could possibly reach any human habitation or activity, I do not shoot at an angle that could ever enter that safety zone. Like all conscientious hunters, we must always be cognizant of the background of every shot, bow or gun.

When I deliver a solid arrow hit on a ground-hugging target like a nut-digging squirrel or a bush-hidden rabbit or gamebird, oftentimes the arrow buries invisibly into the ground beyond the critter, never to be retrieved. And on those hi-flyers in the tree-tops, most shots stick in the tree, sail into the wild blue yonder, or occasionally, hopefully, stick straight up in a visible location to be returned to the quiver. Usually not. With the hi-cost of most arrows these days, that can really slam the old pocketbook pretty hard. That's why I assemble a wastebasket full of used arrows throughout the year to recycle on these crazy smallgame safaris. It's amazing how straight you can bend a nicked and crooked aluminum arrow back to usable straightness with a little extra effort. Bright fletching helps a lot too when its time to find your arrows whether you hit or miss. The old reliable spring loaded Judo heads by Zwickey and GameTracker are a real Godsend, as they tend to stop the arrow much quicker in the vegetation, yet are still good for killing small critters with a solid head or shoulder hit. Be careful though, because even these heads will stick into a tree way up there where we cannot retrieve them. Most of my smallgame arrows are tipped with the same razor-sharp twoblade Nugent Blade Magnus broadhead that I use on all big game hunts. They just get the job done better. I also use the other quality heads in the same 125-grain weights like Muzzy, GameTracker, Rocky Mountain, Wasp, and so many others. Any sharp head will do on smallgame. It's all about stealth, awareness, accuracy, and timing.

Needless to say, bowhunting for these tiny targets is the ultimate challenge of archery accuracy that you will ever experience. It is the mystical creation that God has provided us in its most fascinating display in the wild. To train our historical predator eyes and ears to pick out such amazingly clever and camouflaged animals is quite the trick unto itself. There is no better lesson in level of awareness training than exercising our natural predator instincts and talents. A rabbit or pheasant, squirrel or quail, and of course deer, moose, antelope, and all species, in their natural habitat, are as close to invisible and uncatchable as anything in the world. God created these incredible prey animals specifically to escape with their natural shapes, colors, senses, capabilities, and instincts. Man must be at his very best or absolute luckiest if he hopes to get close to wildlife, much less bring em to bag. Add to this amazing contest the increased demands of hunting with the bow and arrow, and you probably should have your head examined. Maybe chicken isn't that bad of an idea!

Everyday afield is a great reminder of the natural order and how we can better relate to her Tooth, Fang, and Claw reality. I wouldn't be so pompous as to form an "opinion" about nature's rules. I simply bow to her truth and play the game properly. With but a modicum of thought, the truth will settle in the heart. And it is this truth that compels us to participate in this exciting predator/prey contest. And a wild contest it is. It is almost always quick, reflexive shooting at a small spot of an already small target. And is it ever a riot! I learn so much with every moment and every step beyond the pale pavement. Slow and easy with ultracare and awareness is the only way to bring home the bacon. A little prayer every few steps doesn't hurt either.

And it appeared this morning that I better learn to pray a little harder, for the arrogant limbrat continued on his merry, defiant, nut-gathering way as I stood there arrowless, helpless, and laughing at my hopeless display of human failure. This represented the fifth missed squirrel for the morning, and I was tempted to draw my Glock and get even for the dozen arrows they had cost me. But I was laughing too hard, plus the little booger deserved a reprieve. He earned his freedom this day, though one of the many red-tailed hawks, given the shot, would be completely unforgiving and would whack the first one he could get his talons into. I was tempted to stroll the vast sawgrass marsh looking for the arrows sticking straight up out there somewhere, but decided to do so next winter as part of my ritual arrow and shed antler search when the vegetation was dead and down. For now I would just slowly hike back to the truck, stopping every little while, lookin' to the heavens, watching more squirrels do what the cute little acrobatic rodents do, just glad to be alive in a country full of wildlife opportunities limited only by one's imagination and time management priorities. I will have to hurry a bit, because I will have to retrieve some venison from the freezer since there will be no squirrel fricassee on the grill tonight! Maybe tomorrow. I'll go get some more arrows. 🏹

CHAPTER
18

DUCK, DUCK, GOOSE

t's a toss up as to which one of us quivers more uncontrollably, Gonzo the Wonder Lab or ol' ShotGun Slim Guitarboy. My whimpering noises are a bit louder than Gonzo's, but here we sit, shaking like windblown leaves, cold and shivering, looking to the sky for incoming mallards and wood ducks, drooling with anticipation. We always get into the sacred marsh way too early, stumbling through the impenetrable puckerbrush in the pitch black of predawn, damn lucky not to poke out an eye or two and scratch ourselves into a bloody, ripped fleshmess. And of course the flashlite batteries always seem to be on their last flicker, the decoys somehow get tangled up beyond hope, and all my waders appear to be manufactured with a breather hole somewhere in the lower leg region. Are we having fun yet? Thank God for a thermos of hot coffee.

And I've got to tell you, just an hour ago, never has anything in the history of mankind looked so powerfully tempting than my kingsize, firm bed, my beautiful wife Shemane writhing there, purring in the glow of burning logs, all snuggled up in our fluffy down comforter, warm as toast sandwiched in sateen and flannel. With the snot flying outside, cold rain pelting the windows, and the whipping wind howling a primal tune, I must be hopelessly out of my ever lovin' mind to choose the cold, wet, nasty, hellswamp duckmarsh instead of squirming right back into that bed with her. Remind me to have my head examined.

But alas, so goes the addicted waterfowler. We are driven to suck up massive quantities of pungent, stimulating fall air, augmented by the delicious aroma of that black muck that supports sawgrass and cattails; the intense changes in the air have a distinct taste and feel all their own. Add to this intoxicating brew a flight of big quacking greenheads with big orange feet extended overhead, with a hunk of cold blue steel auto 12 in hand, and I'm here to tell ya folks, you got heaven on earth. Better than a hotdog at the baseball game or much else I can think of; a sunrise in wildfowl habitat is one of those moments in life that has a life of its own. Include your son and/or daughter, any loved one or buddy at your side, a stinking, shaking hulk of a duck-radar Labrador retriever, and I'm sorry, it just don't get no better than this.

The first ducks in are usually too early to see, but even these old wounded, abused, rock 'n' roll guitar ears can pick up the incredible swooshing of an incoming woody. Barely a few feet over our heads, the first two or three always surprise us, the dog's ears and head cocking wildly to the sound, and the whimpering sounds increasing. Like tiny fighter jets diving their targets, these beautiful ducks give a little welcoming whistle as they zoom above the marsh. It's wonderful. We just sit back and take it all in.

The amazing numbers of Canada geese these days add a punch of excitement as they announce the eminent light of day with their increasing cackling and honking on every body of water nearby. We double check our right-hand parka pockets and clutch the heavy backup loads of three-inch magnum BBs, hoping the big honkers will fly over our honeyhole this morning for a bonus goose blast. Big Canada decoys float in amongst the assortment of Blackwater duck dekes to sweeten the pot, just in case.

This morning we are using a shield of Fast Grass around our Mossy Oak Avery duckblind, augmented with some Whacker Backer manmade pine boughs and PMI Cover system fake oak leaf limbs to help hide us from prying eyes overhead. These commercial products make it a whole lot easier to fool ducks and geese with their upperhand bird's eye view of the whole shooting match. We even wear Mossy Oak Shadowgrass facemasks to cover our pink faces, the number one danger alert to ultra-wary overhead fowl.

In my fifty-three years, I have never seen more ducks and geese as I have in the past few seasons. And thanks to dedicated hunting organizations like Ducks Unlimited,

GOOSEBREAST RENDEZVOUS

Soak pure, scrumptious goosebreasts in some heavily garlic-peppered apple cider vinegar for a few hours in the fridge, then sear em good and crispy in some ultra HOT olive oil. Add diced white onions and celery for the last minute. Lightly celery salt and garlic salt em. Add a splash of white wine, turn off heat, cover for 2 minutes, then serve with smashed potatoes, and eat naked at the fireplace. Now that's reverence for wildlife! That, my friends, is a Prayer for the WildThings! Say YOWZA and belch loudly! Then shoot more!

Waterfowl USA, and Delta Waterfowl, habitat is improving and bird numbers are stable and rising. Gonzo smiles his approval, and I grab my shotgun a little tighter. It's nearly daylite in the swamp, boys!

We hunker down tight into the leafy blind as a pair of big mallards circle out of range, then cup their wings for a final approach. It's breathtaking. At the universal duckhunter call TAKE EM! guns rise in unison and fire belches skybound. Two unheard reports from the 12-gauges erupt and the two birds fold cleanly and splash in front of the happy hunters. Poor Gonzo is about to explode, and at the command to mark and fetch, he virtually blasts into the pond and handily brings both stunning greenheads to hand with two fine retrieves. All that summertime training has come to fruition, and this old hunter glows with pride. Good Lord, is this cool!

A few more mallards are taken along with our limit of wood ducks, and as we are about to call it a morning, we hear the distant honking of Canadas heading our way. We scramble to regroup, slamming gooseloads into our guns, and replacing facemasks. When our Primos call sings, as if on a tractorbeam direct from the hands of God, four giant Canada geese bear straight down on our little makeshift blind, and as they attempt to sail over, we raise up as if in slomotion and kill all four of em. It was absolutely amazing. One of the great big birds nearly took us out as it crashed into our blind, missing us by inches, only because we dodged the twenty-pound missile of muscle and feathers. We laughed out loud at our good fortune, gathered up our birdy gifts, and sipped the last of our hot mocha from the camo thermos.

Many photos were taken of our memorable, joyous celebration, and then a plucking party ensued in preparation for a feast fit for kings and queens, and of course us knaves as well. Some birds and the geese were breasted, but extra care was taken to thoroughly pluck the biggest and best birds, for there may be no better meal on the planet than fresh roasted wood duck or mallard. And it's a real simple cooking procedure that provides scrumptious chow.

Fresh Roasted Wood Duck

I take nice, fat, clean birds, gut em and wash em thoroughly inside and out, removing every single feather including the nearly invisible pinfeathers and being sure to remove all blood, veins, and inner tissue. I then amply coat the inside with McCormick's garlic salt and garlic pepper, place them in a zipbag, and refrigerate overnite.

Preparing the roasting pan is real easy. I coat the outside of each bird with good cooking oil, even a quality virgin olive oil, adding a light covering of celery salt. I sprinkle a light dusting of parsley flakes over each bird, figuring one bird per diner, and then add a light amount of garlic pepper and garlic salt. In the pan with the ducks I place quartered red potatoes and bite-sized sliced carrots and celery. Then I stick a quarter of green apple in each bird cavity along with a slice of red or white onion. (I prefer the red.) Slices of onion and apple are added randomly to the pan for added flavor and treats. I pour in ¼ cup white wine and ¼ cup water, sprinkle a little garlic pepper and garlic salt over the whole shebang, and slip the covered roastpan in a 350 degree oven for 3 hours. I check it each hour to be sure it cooks to dark brown but not burnt, basting thoroughly each time.

We sit down to dine on this moving feast with nearly the same excitement as the thrill of the duckblind party, and everyone who has ever experienced it expresses lipsmacking, oohing and ahhing joy. A glass of white wine or Vernor's Ginger Ale complements this beggars' banquet, and it's not surprising that everybody wants to know more about ducks and duck hunting, understanding clearly that these precious renewable resources are best respected with a shotgun, a good dog, and a knife and fork.

19

MORE DELICIOUS BIRDING

A s I frolic like a leaping gnome back into the wild again, every day during the sensational season of harvest, each dynamic moment of each and every hunt reminds me how much fun and important this hunting lifestyle is to me. Every breathtaking sunrise explosion, each ear-piquing birdsong, each and every sound, sight, smell, instinct, and feeling that occurs beyond the pavement stimulates my inner soul and the goosebump orgy on my skin. I flatout love this stuff! And it sure doesn't matter whether I'm just out plinking with my .22 revolver; looking to bag a limbrat for the pot; cruising the cattails with the uppity bird-dogs for beautiful, gaudy, ring-necked pheasants; or sneaking beneath the stunning canopy of hardwoods, trusty bow and arrows in hand, trying to outwit the mighty whitetailed deer. My heart patters with excitement like a runaway locomotive about to career off the tracks. I crave it all. Though technology has progressed by leaps and bounds in some ways, in actual tangible functionary pursuits, some things remain the same as when I started hunting back in the early 1950s. We still have to drag our weary bones out of the warm sack for an early start, pay close attention to the powerful forces of nature, and strive for optimal level of awareness to outfox the wary beasts. It doesn't really matter if we have great grandpa's old turn of the century flintlock or some state-of-the-art deluxe sniper rifle in the latest ballistic wildcat; bagging game and having a goodtime still depends on the individual effort and attitude. That's the beauty of hunting, fishing, and trapping. It demands individualism and patience with a good dose of discipline to actually bring things together. It is that challenge that calls so many of us to the wild. That, and the delicious pure sustenance, salmonella-free, sacred protein of Ma Nature's woodland fowl.

Quail Roast

1 quail
1 grape leaf
Salt pork, sliced, enough to cover quail
Butter or margarine
½ cup water
1 tablespoon sherry
¼ cup seedless grapes

Preheat oven to 450 degrees. Heat a shallow pan in oven.
Clean quail and wrap in grape leaf. Cover with slices of
salt pork and tie in place with kitchen string. Place quail,
breast up, in heated pan and spread with butter. Roast
uncovered, basting often, 15 to 20 minutes, depending
on degree of rareness desired. Remove quail from pan,
remove leaf, and place under broiler for a few minutes to
brown. Add water to drippings in pan and simmer to
loosen all bits that cling to pan. Add sherry and seedless
grapes and serve with quail. Allow 1 bird per serving.

Quail in Tomato Sauce

4 quail, skinned, washed, and halved
3 tablespoons margarine
1 medium onion, chopped
½ cup mushrooms, sliced
1 16-ounce can stewed tomatoes
1 teaspoon instant chicken bouillon
1 8-ounce can tomato sauce
1 teaspoon basil

Pat quail dry with a paper towel. In a skillet, melt the margarine, add the quail, and cook until well-browned. Remove quail and use same skillet to brown onion and mushrooms. Add rest of ingredients and stir to mix. Heat to simmer and place quail back in skillet. Spoon sauce over birds, cover, and simmer for about 20 minutes, or until quail are tender. Baste occasionally. If liquid cooks away, lower heat and add a little water. Serve with hot cooked rice or noodles. Serves 4.

Pheasant and Rice

1 cup wild rice, uncooked
1 can cream of chicken soup
1 can cream of mushroom soup
2½ cups water
1 can mushroom stems and pieces
1 can water chestnuts
2 pheasants, cut in pieces, floured, and browned
1 package dry onion soup mix

In a casserole dish, mix all ingredients except pheasant and onion soup mix. Add pheasant and sprinkle onion soup mix over top. Cover loosely with foil and bake for 3 hours at 300 degrees.

Pheasant Hash

¼ cup margarine
2 cups cooked and diced potatoes
2 to 3 cooked and diced pheasant breasts
1 small onion, diced
1 12-ounce can corn niblets
1 teaspoon dried tarragon
½ teaspoon pepper
1 teaspoon dried parsley
1½ teaspoons instant chicken bouillon
¼ cup water
1 10- to 11-ounce can cream of chicken soup
½ cup milk

Melt margarine in a large covered sauté pan or electric frying pan. Add potatoes and brown. Add all remaining ingredients and mix thoroughly. Cover and simmer for 30 minutes, stirring occasionally. Serves 4 to 6.

Pheasant Chow Mein

1 cup chopped onion
1 cup chopped celery
1 pound diced, cooked pheasant
Shortening for frying
1 can bean sprouts
3 tablespoons brown gravy

Brown onions, celery, and pheasant in a sauté pan with a little shortening. Add bean sprouts and gravy and simmer for 1 hour, adding water as needed. Serve with crispy chow mein noodles and rice.

Apple Pheasant Casserole

1 pheasant, dressed and cut into pieces
Seasoned flour
4 tablespoons butter
½ teaspoon salt
½ teaspoon thyme
⅛ teaspoon black pepper
2 large peeled apples
1 cup apple cider
2 tablespoons wine vinegar

Roll pheasant pieces in seasoned flour and brown in butter over medium heat. Evenly distribute pheasant pieces in deep casserole dish and sprinkle with salt, thyme, and pepper. Add apple slices and pour cider and vinegar over all. Bake covered at 350 degrees for 1¼ hours.

Wild Turkey with Morel Sauce

1 wild turkey breast half, skin and bone removed
2 cups milk
1 cup flour
1 teaspoon salt
½ teaspoon paprika
Dash of pepper
8 tablespoons butter
1 cup fresh morels, chopped
2 tablespoons fresh chives, chopped

Cut breast across the grain into ½-inch-thick slices. Place each slice between waxed paper and pound gently with the flat side of a mallet. Transfer slices to an 8" x 12" or 9" x 13" baking dish, add milk, and let stand for 30 minutes at room temperature. Remove slices and reserve milk.

Combine flour, salt, paprika, and pepper in a large plastic baggie. Stir 3 tablespoons of the mixture into the reserved milk. Place turkey slices individually in bag and shake to coat. Melt 4 tablespoons of butter over medium heat in a skillet. Add half of the turkey slices and cook until golden brown and cooked throughout, turning once. Repeat with remaining slices and keep cooked turkey warm in a 175 degree oven.

In a separate skillet, cook morels over medium heat in remaining butter, until tender. Stir in milk mixture and chives and cook until thickened, stirring constantly. Serve morel sauce over turkey breast slices. Serves 4 to 5.

Wild Turkey Lettuce Wraps
by Shemane

I can convert even the most ardent vegetarian with this recipe. I like it because you can let guests make their own wraps. I've never had leftovers when I've served this.

½ pound cooked wild turkey meat
    in medium bite-sized pieces
2 raw carrots, julienned
½ cup bean sprouts
Boston lettuce leaves, separated
1 cucumber, sliced
2 tablespoons peanut satay sauce (available in jars)

Place each item in separate bowls. To assemble 1 wrap: lay down 1 lettuce leaf and place several slices of turkey meat, some carrots, bean sprouts, and cucumbers on top. Spoon peanut satay sauce on top and wrap lettuce leaf. Enjoy!

Every breathtaking sunrise explosion, each ear-piquing birdsong stimulates my inner soul and the goosebump orgy on my skin.

CHAPTER
20

SEXFRIED FISHSLAB

Sex is the first word that comes to mind when trying to describe my annual Nuge Tribe Gonzo Lake bluegill fishfry. It's that damn good. Hot, juicy, firm, undulating, a little greasy. Absolutely deeeelicious! And a damn riot to catch. This feast for the soul runs from early April, just after full thaw when the small front lake begins to warm, through the entire month of July, sometimes into September. It's the only time of year I actually hate rock 'n' roll because it is summertime, and the livin' aint so eazy in between hunting season when I am driven to rockout and tour like a maniac, scaring whitefolk with my oversouled R&B guitarspeak. Damn! But in amongst the throttling sonic bombast spiritual carnage across the hinterland, I do make it a point to get home a few times each week during this fish slamming orgy to clean massive quantities of 'gills, crappie, and hogass bass from our wonderfully productive private lakes at our family home hunting camps.

My kids never learned to fish; they simply wet lines and haul in gargantuan Slabbage from the depths. With ultralite tackle and a slithering of nitecrawlers, itsa cinch. It's too eazy. They're spoiled rotten. Me too.

Any size fish will do. I understand there is a size limit on bass, but call me Rosa Parks with a hook, cuz the smaller the slab, the sweeter the meat. I defy.

Fresh is everything. Catch em, slice em, fry em, and eat em as fast as ya possibly can. We limit our mess haul based on how much we plan to devour at the next sitting and how many we are willing to filet. Did I mention that I am the FiletMaster? I am the FiletMaster. With a foaming bucket of thirty or forty writhing fishies, I run my Accusharp blade sharpener over my small Outdoor Edge filet knife, and all I can say is "stand back." With an assembly line of dedicated scalers at my side, deftly supervised by ScaleMaster Rocco Winchester, ya best don full-face goggles and body armor, for the shit will be flying hither and yon, to and fro, like shrapnel of luv!

With a still squirming scaled gill, head right and down in my left hand, I bonk the nekkid little turd in the head with the handle of my knife to calm em down a bit (Simmer down, smasha!) Then with cool, smooth, precise single-strokes of the narrow blade, I affectionately carve 99 percent of the ultra-yummy flesh from the skeleton, headfirst to the tailfin, following the ribline so close as to shave bone, then I turn the fish over and do the other side the same way. The precious flesh is washed clean in a bucket of clean water, then placed directly into a bowl of icewater. It takes us approximately thirty seconds per fish. All remains go back into the earth as garden mulch or coonbait. And the circle shall not go unbroken. Sing it!

We make the effort to filet even the smallest of fish, even as small as four and five inches. The smaller ones really are better tasting. We waste nothin'. On private lakes, and usually public waterways as well, it is important to remove as many fish each year as possible (to a point, of course) so as to relieve the lake from overpopulation and its resultant abuse and habitat destruction. Without adequate harvest, fish will stunt and disease and wastefully die off. Even the teeniest tiniest fish are kept and tossed onto the shore for vermin, turtles, and birds to eat. I like balance. Itsa beautiful thang.

Then the festivities begin. 🗡

The FiletMaster's Fresh Fish Fry

We take these clean, cold slabs and drown them in a bowl of well-blended milk and egg goop for a few minutes. This dripping glob is then powdered with a 50-50 blend of flour and Drakes FryCrisp batter and augmented a tad with McCormick's garlic pepper and McCormick's garlic salt. They are then slipped into a few inches of hotter than hell oil till golden brown and piled high onto a paper-towel-covered plate. A touch of fresh tartar sauce or fresh mayonnaise and a splash of lemon will make em that much better. When appropriate, consenting adults would do well to dine nekkid. It's an overall sensual stimuli thang.

This wonderful meal has never failed to bring great joy to all who have shared it with us. When Aerosmith is on tour, Joe Perry and Steven Tyler have been known to drive the extra 140 miles to Camp Nuge just to pigout on this very special beggars' banquet of pure, renewable protein from the delicious spring waters of our sacred swamps. I swear they perform with increased attitude so fueled. I know I do.

Any size fish will do.
Catch em, slice em, fry em,
and eat em as fast as
ya possibly can.

21

THE SOUL SANDWICH

or optimum spiritual sustenance, take two thick, fresh, soft, delicious, ultrafibrous slices-o-life and spread a smooth, luscious, swirling wad of tasty adventure on both sides. Include all the intense sunrizes and sunsets you can possibly squeeze in between. Be sure to allow your emotions and feelings to run wild with zero inhibitions so as to experience every sensation the flood of tastes has to offer, letting nary a spit of the good, the bad, or the ugly go uncelebrated. With your awareness soaring, I am confident that you will weed out all the bad and ugly you can, while maximizing the glory of all the good that flows about. Now that's a spread I can sandwich.

To get the most out of this little snack-o-life, we will want to enjoy each bite with our loving family and friends, for as good as life's joys are to munch, each chomp will deliver so much more if we share them with people we care about and who care about us. Smiles are contagious, reciprocal, and cumulative. The more the merrier. Let your tastebuds run wild. Your spirit will follow.

For life-giving protein, I recommend the pure flesh of renewable critter resources that are at their best roasting above a bed of red woodcoals, sizzling away with robust, stimulating aromas. This maincourse in our soul sandwich will come best handson from a daily exploration into the beautiful unpaved critterzones of the world, where the Great Spirit of the Wild runs strong and free. Where we hunt, fish, and trap, we will celebrate the wild, her creatures, and the very source of our basic quality of life, for as goes the habitat for wildlife, so goes the productivity of our air, soil, and water quality—hence, the very best livable life itself. You may want to stack the meat as high as a Carnegie Deli pastrami mountainwich for best results.

Meat. It's the good food.

Note that it is not the meat itself that buoys the spirit, but rather the system by which we chase down the beast to procure the flesh that truly drives the honesty of our life's reality. No tuna salad ever made it to the bowl without a knife and a gutpile. Know it, love it, admit it, eat it, and celebrate this truism of life, for death begets life and the circle must not and cannot be broken. To deny it and pretend otherwise is foolish and ultimately disrespectful to the beasts and to God. And it's damn stupid.

When one hunts and fishes, we perform a pivotal and natural role and duty in creation, truly benefiting the web of life and indeed the balance of wildlife. To think otherwise is rude. And it is the encounter on hallowed wild ground under these powerful and natural life and death relationships that truly inspires a respect for all life, for to witness the death of one's own food will stay with you always and reside deep in your heart, and you will know intuitively that this food-gathering is serious business.

Fun, but deadly serious. It is the chill and nerve-wracking heartslam that is unique to a wild animal encounter that gives fire to our existence. Something extremely pleasant erupts within us that causes great happiness and anxiousness. When we harvest surplus critters to feed our family, we learn quickly that health and balance is the result, thereby insuring future encounters and unlimited food. That is what drives a reasoning predator, and I for one am damn proud to be one. Like they say, ya can't grill it till ya kill it. I do, therefor I am.

Since we are born at point A and will inevitably perish at point B, dammit, I emphatically repeat: LIV IT UP with all the intellect, attitude, spirit, goodwill, and clever strategizing you can muster. Our soul sandwich should be made from all natural ingredients, well thought out and put together individually so we know exactly what goes into it and our belly. Whole foods or no food at all, I always say. I for one cannot imagine allowing any poisons anywhere near my sandwich or life. For fifty-three ultrafunlovin' greazy all-American rock 'n' roll throbbing years, I have avoided the sense-dulling and tastebud-destroying bullshit of drugs, alcohol, and tobacco, like the imbecilic plague that they are. Why on God's good green earth anyone would knowingly and intentionally ingest substances that guarantee the reduction of one's awareness and sensual radar is way beyond me. Last time I checked, losing touch, puking, and dying a party don't make.

Conversely, by making optimum health job number one, we will be better prepared and equipped to live each day to the fullest, attaining great joy and happiness in our American Dream. Each meal should be a major ThanXGiving gitdown party, showing grand appreciation for these amazing gifts.

Consider each meal another bite into our Soul Sandwich, taking care to savor each and every big and little flavor it has to offer. Miss nothing, waste nothing. Life is a meal. Eat hardy. Savor. 🏹

Here are the first run lyrics to a new song of mine expected to be recorded for a new SpitFire CD in 2002. This tune represents lyrically how I feel about everything, including how I eat and live.

CRAVE

A simple life, I will not have. It doesn't satisfy me.
I don't believe in the status quo,
it kinda leaves me weak. A mountain high
is what I climb, I swim the river deep.
If you crave the time of your life,
try to keep up with me. I'm gonna live,
I'm gonna fly, I'm gonna soar till the day I die.
On the wings of a bird of prey, hey, hey, hey,
you're absolutely what I crave.
Well look at me, that's a smile on my face,
you know it don't come cheap.
Sure I live the American Dream,
go ahead and crucify me.
I'm gonna live, I'm gonna fly,
I'm gonna soar till the day I die.
On the wings of a bird of prey, hey, hey, hey,
you're absolutely what I crave.

(copyright Ted Nugent BroadHead Music 2002)

HEARTY HUNTING SOULFOOD

I will not go like the buffalo.
Nobody can track me down.
I'll make my stand like that buffalo,
but make my way to a higher ground.
The people came from afar away,
they brought the plow and the will to stay.
They broke the ground and their promises,
now we pray for a brand new day.
What would you do for the buffalo?
Sacrifice everything you own?
Give up your life and security,
would you give them back their home?
Don't pretend that they disappeared.
We killed em off with electricity.
Now they're back on a sacred ground,
and we celebrate that the spirit is free.
We got the Spirit of the buffalo, Spirits of the buffalo,
the Spirit is the buffalo.

Those words are the lyrics to my (our) song of survival, "THE SPIRIT OF THE BUFFALO" that came pouring forth outta my guts one morning with son Rocco Winchester in our living room. Upon completion of our daily chores TOGETHER with breakfast dishes, house cleaning, guitar lesson, a little archery, maybe some .22 marksmanship practice, and cleaning, shoveling, and grooming the animals and such, we gazed out onto our beautiful, shining lake—the colorful, flitting songbirds coming and going to our feeders and cornpile, the numerous pairs of squawking geese and boisterous sandhill cranes, and the always inspiring parade of deer across the south ridge. With the spirit all around and within, young Rocco once again recommended we strike up a new song, and the guitar riffs and words flowed as if they had been deeply thought about and previewed for days, when, in fact, they gushed forth spontaneously, motivated by the father-son connection of co-independence and love that we celebrated.

Co-independence. Individual in our decision making, but cognizant of our duty to family and heartfelt desires to benefit community. We can indulge in modern cush comfort and convenience, but I for one would never allow myself to become reliant upon any of it. As we seek to "live simpler so others can simply live," conservation, recycling, and awareness to wasteful cause-and-effect become priority. I didn't wait for Y2K paranoiacs to scare me into firewood stashes and MRE stockpiles. I've always had a few months supply of firewood for our woodstoves and a generator with supplies of fuel, food, and other life support basics on hand. Ever heard of ice storms and tornadoes?

The last Boy Scouts are alive and well and always prepared at Camp Nuge, fully independent at home on the goodship Common

Sense Survival. We live on many wild acres of fuel-producing timber and our three lakes are all springfed for limitless quality water availability. Our entire home compound is 100 percent self-sufficient and can operate indefinitely regardless of how much techno bullshit turns against their masters. Fortunately, my daddy taught and impressed upon me that a goodman can and oughtta stand alone, but his level of awareness and survival skills must be channeled to assist others, within reason.

Water, shelter, heat, and food, and the WILL TO SURVIVE. That's it, kids. Along with those life and death determinates, basic first-aid knowledge and supplies can save lives as well, for in a truly independent situation, you will be on your own. Basic CPR, being able to stop bleeding, and the Heimlich maneuver must be known, plus other rudimentary procedures. Along with firearms and ammo access and understanding, safety, wildlife history, the horrific lessons of the Holocaust, and the rape of the American Indian, I for one cannot believe our school systems do not teach these basics of life as standard, required learning. Go figure. So we parents should make up for the apparent failures. If one fails to grasp the lessons of historical calamities, one is destined to relive them.

The simplest of meat preservation is still the salting, smoking, drying methods of the brave, independent natives, pioneers, trappers, and hunters who settled this wild new America, clearly with a powerful will to survive.

Spread the word—MEAT IS LIFE!

As has been my modus operandi for many wondrous, throbbing years, prioritize on upgrade and recruitment to the side of truth. The good hunting truth and the God-given right to keep and bear arms truth. All else is secondary and pivotal upon these right-to-life basics. For if we can't eat or defend ourselves, how are we to celebrate that which our Creator bestowed upon us— the self-evident truth that we have the right to life, liberty, and the pursuit of happiness? The right to life must mean not dying, not starving, and not being the victim of a bad guy. That spells out irrefutably the right to life the way I see it. Cherish these rights. Live these rights. Hunting is not a privilege. Eating is not a privilege. Surviving an encounter with a paroled murderer is no privilege. These are all God-given rights.

So the next time you're in the midst of a savage Nor'easter, batten down the hatches, stoke up the fire, dream of hunting adventures, and spoon up some delicious, bubbling SoulFood for your Tribe. 🏹

Hunter's Stew

Here at the Nugent Ranch we prepare smashed potatoes with the skins on. Waste nothing!

1 pound ground venison
1 to 2 cups fresh mushrooms
1 can cream of mushroom soup
Smashed potatoes (prepared as you like)

Place venison and mushrooms in a large skillet and cook till brown and tender. Drain, reserving grease for your hunting dogs. Add cream of mushroom soup and mix well. Pour meat mixture over smashed potatoes and serve. Best when coming in from the cold!

Bubble Bean Piranha à la Colorado Moose

This is it, folks! The chow the whole world has been waitin' for! Proven at the hands of the most voracious of camp hogs, this rib-stickin' slop is the ultimate in hunt camp fortification. As the primary mainstay at the Nugent Whackmaster Headquarters, many a hearty hunter has maintained the killer instinct by gettin' a belly full of my primo-extremo brew. First experimented with as early as 1968, the recipe has changed little over the years, but rather improved with the spirit of adventure.

1 pound ground venison (any)
2 green peppers, diced
2 red peppers, diced
1 large sweet onion, peeled and diced
1 large white onion, peeled and diced
1 bunch scallions, trimmed and diced
1 large bowl fresh mushrooms, diced
1 whole clove garlic, peeled and squashed
1 box of elbow macaroni (Creamettes) or shell pasta
1 side deer backstrap, cut into bite-sized pieces
¼ cup olive oil
Splash of white vinegar
Cayenne pepper to taste
Mrs. Dash seasoning to taste
½ pound butter

Brown the ground meat in a large skillet. Add half of the peppers, onions, scallions, and mushrooms to the browned meat. Add the garlic and stir vigorously.

Boil the pasta and drain. Add butter.

In a separate skillet, sear the backstrap pieces in the olive oil and wine vinegar. Throw the whole load into a large pot including cayenne pepper, Mrs. Dash seasoning, and the remaining raw vegetables. Stir in small amounts of water to desired consistency and let simmer over lowest heat all day. Refrigerate leftovers overnight and reheat and eat for days to come. This dish is best 2 to 3 days old. Slop a load onto bread, smashed potatoes, rice, or serve by itself. Throw a log on the fire, kick back, relax, and swap hunting lies. Serves about 5 average, or 2 major, swine.

Curried Pheasant Stew
by Shemane

I must have been Indian in another life because I really enjoy Indian spices and the sweet and hot tastes of many traditional Indian dishes. This one combines an unusual but wonderful combination of raisins and fowl. YUM!

1 tablespoon vegetable oil
1 medium yellow onion, chopped
1 pound pheasant, cubed
1 tablespoon fresh ginger, peeled and minced
4 garlic cloves, minced
1 tablespoon curry powder
1 teaspoon ground cumin
1 teaspoon salt
½ cup water
1 small head cauliflower, trimmed and chopped
3 to 5 carrots, cut lengthwise, then in half
¼ teaspoon ground cayenne pepper
½ cup golden raisins
½ cup fresh cilantro, chopped
1 can stewed tomatoes
Jasmine rice

Heat oil in a nonstick pan over medium heat. Add onion and cook for a few minutes until translucent, stirring occasionally. Increase temperature to medium-high, add pheasant, and cook approximately 5 minutes or until meat is lightly browned on the outside. Then add remaining ingredients except for raisins, cilantro, and tomatoes. Heat to boiling, then reduce to low, cover, and simmer. Add raisins, cilantro, and tomatoes and simmer for just a few more minutes. Serve over hot jasmine rice.

Santa Fe Soup

1 pound ground beast
1 tablespoon oil
½ onion chopped
1 10-ounce can Ro-Tel chili tomatoes, diced
1 pound Velveeta cheese, diced
1 16-ounce can corn
1 16-ounce can pinto beans
1 16-ounce can diced tomatoes

In a large pot, brown ground beast and onion with oil. Drain off oil and add chili tomatoes and cheese. When cheese starts to melt, add the corn, pinto beans (with liquid), and tomatoes and heat through. Serve with tortilla chips on the side.

Pumpkin Goulash
by Shemane

Over the years we have been blessed with the opportunity to travel to Africa, where I was served this meal by an African tribe. The Africans do a lot of cooking outdoors, and after the cooks are finished serving breakfast, they begin to prepare dinner, and they leave it cooking over hot coals for most of the day. They cooked in pots and pans, but they also used large squash and pumpkins. This particular meal was one of my favorites.

1 large pumpkin
2 teaspoons salt
Cooking oil
1 medium onion, chopped
1 pound ground venison
1 cup wild rice, cooked
3 eggs, beaten
¼ cup cream
1 teaspoon sage
¼ teaspoon pepper

Preheat oven to 350 degrees or prepare to cook in an outdoor firepit.

Cut the top from the pumpkin; remove seeds and strings. Prick cavity with a fork and rub with 1 teaspoon of salt.

Pumpkin Goulash (continued)

Heat the oil in a large skillet over medium-high heat. Cook the onion in the oil for 3 to 5 minutes, then add the meat and cook until browned. Remove from heat and stir in wild rice, eggs, cream, sage, pepper, and remaining salt. Pour into pumpkin. Place pumpkin in a shallow baking pan with ¼-inch of water and bake in the oven for 1½ hours OR wrap in foil and cook over hot coals for 2 to 4 hours. Cut pumpkin into wedges and serve with goulash.

Stoke up the fire, dream
of hunting adventures,
and spoon up some
delicious, bubbling
SoulFood for your Tribe.
Spread the word—
MEAT IS LIFE!

APPENDIX
Hunting and Conservation Groups

Buckmasters
10350 Highway 80 East
Montgomery, AL 36117
Phone: (334) 215-3337
Fax: (334) 215-3535
www.buckmasters.com

The CAMOKIDZ Program
390 Marshall St.
Paxton, MA 01612-1228
camokidz@bigbuckclub.com

Delta Waterfowl Foundation
1305 East Central Avenue or P.O. Box 3128
Bismarck, ND 58502
Phone: (888) 987-3695
E-mail: usa@deltawaterfowl.org
www.deltawaterfowl.org

Ducks Unlimited, Inc.
One Waterfowl Way
Memphis, TN 38120
Phone: (800) 45DUCKS or (901) 758-3825
www.ducks.org

Foundation for Blacktail Deer
c/o Wilderness Sound Productions
4015 Main St., Suite A
Springfield, OR 97478
Phone: (541) 741-0263
E-mail: info@blacktail.org
www.blacktail.org

Foundation for North American Wild Sheep
P.O. Box 146
Douglas, WY 82633-0146
Phone: (307) 358-3693
Fax: (307) 358-3262
www.fnaws.org

Gun Owners of America
8001 Forbes Place, Suite 102
Springfield, VA 22151
Phone: (703) 321-8585
Fax: (703) 321-8408
www.gunowners.org

International Bowhunting Organization
P.O. Box 398
Vermilion, OH 44089
Phone: (440) 967-2137
www.ibo.net

Michigan United Conservation Clubs
P.O. Box 30235
Lansing, MI 48909
Phone: (517) 371-1041 or (800) 777-6720
www.mucc.org

National Field Archery Association
31407 Outer I-10
Redlands, CA 92373
Phone: (909) 794-2133 or (800) 811-2331
Fax: (909) 794-8512
E-mail: NFAArchery@aol.com
www.nfaa-archery.org

National Trapper's Association
P.O. Box 3667
Bloomington, IL 61702
E-mail: trappers@aol.com
www.nationaltrappers.com

National Wild Turkey Federation
P.O. Box 530
Edgefield, SC 29824
Phone: (803) 637-3106 or (800) THE-NWTF
Fax: (803) 637-0034
E-mail: nwtf@nwtf.net
www.nwtf.com

North American Waterfowl Federation
nawf@up-north.com
www.nawf.org

Pheasants Forever
1783 Buerckle Circle
St. Paul, MN 55110
Phone: (651) 773-2000
Fax: (651) 773-5500
www.pheasantsforever.org

Quail Unlimited National Headquarters
31 Quail Run or P.O. Box 610
Edgefield, SC 29824
Phone: (803) 637-5731
Fax: (803) 637-0037
www.qu.org

Rocky Mountain Elk Foundation
2291 W. Broadway or P.O. Box 8249
Missoula, MT 59807
Phone: (800) CALL-ELK (225-5355)
Fax: (406) 523-4500
E-mail: info@rmef.org
www.rmef.org

Ruffed Grouse Society, Inc.
451 McCormick Road
Coraopolis, PA 15108
Phone: (412) 262-4044
Fax: (412) 262-9207
RGS@ruffedgrousesociety.org
www.ruffedgrousesociety.org

Safari Club International
4800 West Gates Pass Road
Tucson, AZ 85745
Phone: (520) 620-1220
Fax: (520) 622-1205
www.safariclub.org

Trout Unlimited
1500 Wilson Blvd., #310
Arlington, VA 22209-2404
Phone: (703) 522-0200
Fax: (703) 284-9400
E-mail: trout@tu.org
www.tu.org

U.S. Sportsmen's Alliance
[Formerly the Wildlife Legislative Fund of America (WLFA)]
801 Kingsmill Parkway
Columbus, OH 43229
Phone: (614) 888-4868
E-mail: info@ussportsmen.org
www.wlfa.org

Varmint Hunters Association, Inc.
P.O. Box 759
Pierre, SD 57501
Phone: (605) 224-6665
Fax: (605) 224-6544
www.varminthunter.org

Waterfowl U.S.A.
Box 50
The Waterfowl Building
Edgefield, SC 29824
Phone: (803) 637-5767
Fax: (803) 637-6983
www.waterfowlusa.org

Whitetails Forever Network
P.O. Box 99
Ithaca, MI 48847
Phone: (989) 875-2996
Fax: (989) 875-8533
www.whitetailsforevernetwork.com

Whitetails Unlimited
P.O. Box 720 or 1715 Rhode Island Street
Sturgeon Bay, WI 54235
Phone: (920) 743-6777 or (800) 274-5471
Fax: (920) 743-4658
E-mail: wtu@itol.com
www.whitetailsunlimited.org

RECIPE INDEX